THE INFINITE WEALTH MINDSET

UNVEILING
THE SPIRITUAL AND MENTAL PATH
TO INFINITE WEALTH

(EXTENDED EDITION)

-

WRITTEN BY
NEVILLE GODDARD

The Infinite Wealth Mindset - Unveiling The Spiritual And Mental Path To Infinite Wealth (Extended Edition)
By Neville Goddard

CONTENT

ABOUT THIS BOOK

This book is a public domain ebook, enriched with new content that delves into the life and teachings of the original author. The additional material serves as an insightful expansion, designed to provide readers with a deeper understanding of the context surrounding the author's work. By incorporating details about the author's life and the philosophical underpinnings of their teachings, this enhanced edition offers a comprehensive exploration that goes beyond the original text. Readers are invited to engage with a more comprehensive narrative, gaining not only knowledge of the author's literary contributions but also a nuanced perspective on the factors that influenced their work.

BRIEF BOOK INTRODUCTION

"The Infinite Wealth Mindset" is an extraordinary book that invites readers on a profound journey into the teachings of Neville Goddard. Centered around a lecture that has now become part of the public domain, this book presents an invaluable opportunity to explore the transformative insights and profound wisdom of Goddard.

"The Infinite Wealth Mindset" is not merely a book; it is a guide that opens the door to a deeper understanding of spirituality and personal growth. As readers embark on this journey, they are encouraged to reflect on their own lives and contemplate the profound implications of Goddard's teachings. Through introspection and application, readers can harness the power of prayer and manifestation to create positive change in their lives.

BRIEF BIOGRAPHY
OF NEVILLE GODDARD

INTRODUCTION

Neville Goddard (1905-1972) was a profound spiritual teacher and author whose teachings continue to inspire and transform countless lives to this day. Born in Barbados and later immigrating to the United States, Goddard dedicated his life to unraveling the mysteries of consciousness, imagination, and the power of prayer. His profound insights and teachings have made a lasting impact on the fields of metaphysics, spirituality, and personal development.

EARLY LIFE AND AWAKENING

Neville Goddard, originally named Neville Lancelot Goddard, was born on February 19, 1905, in St. Michael, Barbados. As a young man, he migrated to New York City, seeking opportunities and a new life. It was during this time that he encountered a series of mystical experiences that would forever shape his path.
Goddard's Awakening occurred after attending a lecture by the Ethiopian mystic Abdullah. In this transformative encounter, he realized the power of his own consciousness and imagination to shape his reality. This revelation sparked a deep curiosity and ignited a lifelong exploration into the nature of human consciousness and its relationship to the world.

TEACHINGS AND PHILOSOPHY

Goddard's core teachings revolved around the concepts of imagination, assumption, and the power of consciousness. He believed that every individual possessed the innate ability to manifest their desires through the deliberate use of their imagination. According to Goddard, imagination was the creative force that shaped our reality, and by assuming the feeling of our desired outcome already fulfilled, we could bring it into our physical experience.

His lectures and books emphasized the importance of self-reflection, self-awareness, and the conscious use of mental imagery. Goddard believed that individuals had the power to manifest their dreams and aspirations by aligning their thoughts, feelings, and beliefs with the desired outcome.

NOTABLE WORKS AND LEGACY

Throughout his life, Neville Goddard delivered countless lectures and wrote numerous books, which continue to be celebrated for their profound wisdom and practical application. Some of his notable works include "The Power of Awareness," "Feeling is the Secret," "The Law and the Promise," and "Awakened Imagination."

Goddard's teachings have influenced spiritual leaders, authors, and thinkers across the globe. His unique approach to metaphysics and the power of consciousness has resonated with individuals seeking personal transformation and a deeper understanding of their role in creating their reality.

ABOUT NEVILLE GODDARD

Neville Goddard was a mystic and spiritual teacher who lived from 1905 to 1972. He was born in Barbados and later moved to New York City, where he began to study spiritual and mystical teachings. He also studied the work of psychologists such as Sigmund Freud and Carl Jung.

Goddard's main teachings focus on the power of the imagination to create one's reality. He believed that everything in our lives, from our circumstances to our health, is a result of our imaginal acts. He taught that by changing our thoughts and beliefs, we can change our lives and manifest our desires.

One of Goddard's unique concepts is that of the "law of assumption". He believed that whatever we assume to be true about ourselves and our lives, we will experience. This is because our assumptions shape our beliefs, which in turn shape our reality. Goddard taught that by assuming the feeling of our desired outcome, we can bring it into manifestation.

Another important concept in Goddard's teachings is that of the "state akin to sleep". He believed that in order to create our desired reality, we must enter into a relaxed, receptive state similar to sleep. In this state, we can use our imagination to visualize our desires as already manifested, and thus bring them into physical reality.

Goddard also taught that we are all one consciousness, and that the physical world is an illusion created by our collective consciousness. He believed that by changing our consciousness, we can change the world around us.

In terms of practical advice, Goddard emphasized the importance of focusing on our desired outcome and ignoring any negative thoughts or beliefs that might contradict it. He also stressed the need to cultivate a deep sense of gratitude for what we already have, as this creates a positive energy that attracts more of what we desire.

Neville Goddard's teachings have had a profound impact on the field of metaphysics and the study of consciousness. His emphasis on the power of the imagination and the law of assumption have inspired countless individuals to take control of their lives and create their own reality.

FUNDAMENTALS

"It is your state of consciousness that attracts your life." by Neville Goddard

From New Thought, the International New Thought Alliance Bulletin, summer, 1953

I have edited this article slightly, to make it more readable. My own
comments are underlined. -AD WITH so vast a subject, it is indeed a difficult task to summarize in a few hundred words what I consider the most basic ideas on which those who seek a true understanding of [practical, applied] metaphysics should now concentrate. I shall do what I can in the shape of three fundamentals. These fundamentals are:

1. Self-Observation;
2. Definition of Aim;
3. Detachment.

First Fundamental: Self-Observation

The purpose of true metaphysics is to bring about a rebirth or radical psychological change in the individual. Such a change cannot take place until the individual first discovers the self that he would change. This discovery can be made only through a careful observation of his reactions to life. The sum total of these reactions defines the individual's state of consciousness, and it is the individual's state of consciousness that attracts the situations and circumstances of his life.

So the starting point of true metaphysics, on its practical side, is self-observation
in order to discover one's reactions to life, reactions which form one's secret self – the cause of the phenomena of life.

Note that the deeper, "secret", self that Neville is talking about is the deepest personal or individual self, and not the ultimate, universal, formless self. Neville is thus referring to our deepest— and often buried and unconscious—self-concepts, not our ultimate true Self, which is conceptless.

With Emerson, I accept the fact that "Man surrounds himself with the true image
of himself . . . what we are, that only can we see."

There is a definite connection between what is outer and what is inner in man,
and it is ever our inner states that attract our outer life. Therefore, the individual
must always start with himself.

It is one's self that must be changed.

Man, in his blindness, is quite satisfied with himself, but heartily dislikes the circumstances and situations of his life. He feels this way, not knowing that the cause of his displeasure lies not in the condition nor the person with whom he is displeased, but in the very self he likes so much. Not realizing that "he surrounds himself with the true image of himself" and that "what he is, that only can he see," he is shocked when he discovers that it has always been his own deceitfulness that made him suspicious of others.

Self-observation would reveal this deceitful one in all of us; and this one must be accepted before there can be any transformation of ourselves.

At this moment, try to notice your inner state. To what thoughts are you consenting? With what feelings are you identified? You must be ever careful where you are within yourself.

Most of its think that we are kind and loving, generous and tolerant, forgiving and noble; but a careful observation of our reactions to life will reveal a self that is not at all kind and loving, generous and tolerant, forgiving and noble. And it is this self that we must first accept and then set about to change.

Note what Neville is emphasizing here. If we want to become the person we always wanted to be, we must first accept what we are now, even if we don't like it, even if it scares and repulses us. Don't suppress self-awareness, driving it deeper into unconsciousness, just because you don't like it. Don't ignore it, look straight at it. And don't try to change it before you have fully accepted it. Remember this principle of our course: Whatever you are, at any time in your life, is perfect. Why? Because God, Being, is perfect and all-in-all. Part of the great illusion is that there are imperfect and evil beings in the real world.

Rebirth depends on inner work on one's self. No one can be reborn without changing this self. Any time that an entirely new set of reactions enters into a person's life, a change of consciousness has taken place, a spiritual rebirth has occurred.

Second Fundamental: Definition of Aim

Having discovered, through a careful observation of your reactions to life, a self that must be changed, you must now formulate an aim. That is, you must define the one you would like to be instead of the one you truly are in secret. With this aim clearly defined, you must, throughout your conscious waking day, notice your every reaction in regard to this aim.

The reason for this is that everyone lives in a definite state of consciousness, which state of consciousness we have already described as the sum total of his reactions to life. Therefore, in defining an aim, you are defining a state of consciousness, which, like all states of consciousness, must have its reactions to life. For example: if a rumor or an idle remark could cause an anxious reaction in one person and no reaction in another, this is positive proof that the two people are living in two different states of consciousness.

If you define your aim as a noble, generous, secure, kindly individual—knowing that all things are states of consciousness—you can easily tell whether you are faithful to your aim in life by watching your reactions to the daily events of life. If you are faithful to your ideal, your reactions will conform to your aim, for you will be identified with your aim and, therefore, will be thinking from your aim. If your reactions are not in harmony with your ideal, it is a sure sign that you are separated from your ideal and are only thinking of it. Assume that you are the loving one you want to be, and notice your reactions throughout the day in regard to that assumption; for your reactions will tell you the state from which you are operating.

Third Fundamental: Detachment

This is where the third fundamental—detachment—enters in. Having discovered that everything is a state consciousness made visible and having defined that particular state which we want to make visible, we now set about the task of entering such a state, for we must move psychologically from where we are to where we desire to be.

The purpose of practicing detachment is to separate us from our present reactions to life and attach us to our aim in life. This inner separation must be developed by practice. At first we seem to have no power to separate ourselves from undesirable inner states, simply because we have always taken every mood, every reaction, as natural and have become identified with them. When we have no idea that our reactions are only states of consciousness from which it is possible to separate ourselves, we go round and round in the same circle of problems – not seeing them as inner states but as outer situations. We practice detachment, or inner separation, that we may escape from the circle of our habitual reactions to life. That is why we must formulate an aim and constantly notice ourselves in regard to that aim.

This teaching begins with self-observation. Secondly it asks, "What do you want?" And then it teaches detachment from all negative states and attachment to your aim. This last state—attachment to your aim—is accomplished by frequently assuming the feeling of your wish fulfilled.

We must practice separating ourselves from our negative moods and thoughts in the midst of all the troubles and disasters of daily life. No one can be different from what he is now unless he begins to separate himself from his present reactions and to identify himself with his aim. Detachment from negative states and assumption of the wish fulfilled must be practiced in the midst of all the
blessings and cursings of life.

Note that detachment and separation from our undesired states and assumption of the kind of person we always wanted to be is an example of what Shinn called "the law of substitution".

By "assumption" Neville means "taking for granted", in our imagination, frequently during the day and especially at sensitive times—like when we are drifting into sleep at night—definite images and feelings of who we always wanted to be.

The way of true metaphysics lies in the midst of all that is going on in life. We must constantly practice self-observation, thinking from our aim, and detachment from negative moods and thoughts if we would be doers of truth instead of mere hearers.

Practice these three fundamentals and you will rise to higher and higher levels of consciousness. Remember, always, it is your state of consciousness that attracts your life.

Start climbing!

Neville

LESSONS FROM THE LECTURE

1. CONSCIOUSNESS ATTRACTS LIFE:
Neville Goddard emphasizes that our state of consciousness is the primary force that attracts the situations and circumstances in our life. Understanding this fundamental concept is crucial in practical metaphysics.

2. SELF-OBSERVATION:
Self-observation is the starting point for personal transformation. To change, one must first discover their current state of consciousness by carefully observing their reactions to life events. This self-awareness is essential for growth.

3. DEEPER SELF-CONCEPT:
Neville differentiates between the surface self that we often project and our deeper, often unconscious, self-concept. True transformation requires acknowledging and accepting this deeper self, even if it contradicts our ideal self-image.

4. ACCEPTANCE BEFORE CHANGE:
Before attempting any change, it is crucial to fully accept and acknowledge one's current state, even if it is unpleasant or uncomfortable. Suppression or denial of this self-concept can hinder progress.

5. REBIRTH THROUGH INNER WORK:
Neville suggests that rebirth or significant psychological change occurs through inner work. When an entirely new set of reactions and perspectives enter our life, it signifies a spiritual rebirth. This transformation is only possible through self-awareness and change at the deepest level.

6. DEFINITION OF AIM:
To transform, one must clearly define the person they aspire to become. This defined aim represents a specific state of consciousness that guides reactions to life events. It is vital to be faithful to this ideal in thought and action.

7. ALIGNMENT WITH AIM:
One can gauge their progress by observing how well their reactions align with their defined aim. Consistency between reactions and the ideal state of consciousness indicates alignment, while inconsistency reveals a disconnect from the desired self.

8. DETACHMENT:
Detachment involves separating from negative or undesirable inner states and attaching oneself to the desired aim. This practice allows individuals to break free from habitual reactions to life's challenges and move closer to their goals.

9. THE LAW OF SUBSTITUTION:
Neville mentions the law of substitution, which involves replacing negative thoughts and emotions with positive ones. This practice reinforces detachment from negative states and reinforces the assumption of the desired self.

10. PRACTICE AMIDST LIFE'S CHALLENGES:
Neville emphasizes that the path to personal transformation lies in the midst of life's ups and downs. Self-observation, alignment with the defined aim, and detachment must be practiced consistently, regardless of external circumstances.

CHANGING THE FEELING OF "I"

Neville Goddard 1953

For the benefit of those who were not present last Sunday, just let me give you a quick summary of the thought expressed here. We claimed that the world was a manifestation of consciousness, that the individual's environment, circumstances and conditions of life were only the out picturing of the particular state of consciousness in which that individual abides. Therefore, the individual sees whatever he is by virtue of the state of consciousness from which he views the world. Any attempt to change the outer world before he changes the inner structure of his mind, is to labor in vain. Everything happens by order. Those who help or hinder us, whether they know it or not, are the servants of that law, which constantly shapes outward circumstances in harmony with our inner nature. We asked you last Sunday to distinguish between the individual identity and the state the occupy. The individual identity is the Son of God. It is that I speak of you or to you, or speak of myself, I mean really our imagination. That is permanent. It fuses with state and believes itself to be the state with which it is fused, but at every moment of time it is free to choose the state with which it will be identified.

And that brings us to today's subject, "Changing the Feeling of I", and I hope I will not get the same reaction that is recorded in the sixth chapter of the Gospel of John. For we are told that when this was given to the world they all left him, leaving just a handful behind. For when he told them there was no one to change but self, they said this is a hard, hard teaching. It's a hard thing. Who can hear it? For he said, "No man cometh unto me save I call him."

And then it's recorded when he repeated it three times they left him, never again to walk with him. And he turned to the few who remained and asked them, "Would you also go?" And they answered and said, "To whom would we go ? You have the word of eternal life. 'I In other words, it's so much easier when I can blame another for my misfortune, but now that I am told that no man cometh unto me save I call him, that I am the sole architect of my fortunes and misfortunes, it's a difficult saying, and so it's recorded "It's a hard saying. Who can hear it? Who can grasp it? And who will believe it?" And so he said, "And now I sanctify myself that they also be sanctified through the truth, for if this is the truth, then there is no one to change, no one to make whole, no one to purify but self."

And so we start with the "I" . Most of us are totally unaware of the self that we really cherish. We have never taken one good look at the self, so we don't know this self, for the "I" has neither face, form nor figure, but it does mold itself into structure by all that it consents to, all that it believes, and few of us know really what we do believe. We have no idea of the unnumbered superstitions and prejudices that go to mold this inner, formless "I" into a form which is then projected as a man's environment, as the conditions of life.

So here, read it carefully when you go home, "No man cometh unto me save I call him. You didn't choose me; I have chosen you. No man can take away my life; I lay it down myself . There is no power to take from me anything that is part of the inner arrangement of my mind.

All that you gave me I have kept and none is lost save the son of perdition or the belief in God, and because nothing can be lost but the belief in loss, I will not now assume loss of anything you have given me that is good. And so I sanctify myself that they be sanctified through the truth".

And now, how do we go about changing the "I". First of all, we must discover the "I" and we do this by an uncritical observation of self. This will reveal a self that will shock you. You will be altogether, I wouldn't say afraid, but ashamed to admit you've ever known such a lowly creature. And had it been God Himself who drew near in this despicable form, you would have denied him a thousand times before a single cock would crow. You couldn't believe that this is the self that you've carried around and protected and excused and justified. Then you start changing this self after, by an uncritical observation, you make the discovery of that self. For the acceptance of self is the essence of the moral problem of the world. It is the epitome of a true outlook on life, for it is the sole cause of everything you observe.

Your description of the world is a confession of the self that you do not know. You describe another, you describe society, you describe anything, and your description of the thing you observe reveals to one who knows this law the being you really are. So you must first accept that self. When that self is accepted, then you can start to change. It's so much easier to take the virtues of the Gospel and apply them as the word of life, to love the enemy, to bless those who curse us, and to feed the hungry.

But when man discovers the being to be fed, the being to be clothed, the being to be sheltered, the greatest enemy of all is that self, then he is ashamed, completely ashamed that that is the being, for it was easier to share with another something that I possess, to take an extra coat and give it to another, but when I know the truth it's not that. I start with the self, having discovered, and start with change of that self.

Now, let me tell you a story. A few years ago in this city I was giving a series of lectures down near that lake - I can't even recall the name of the lake but it was some Parkview Manor was the place where I spoke, and in that audience was a gentleman who sought an audience before the meeting. And we went across the street into the little park there, and he said to me that he had an insoluble problem. I said, "There is no such thing as an insoluble problem. "But", he said, "you do not know my problem. It's not a state of health, I assure you; it is look at the skin that I wear" . I said, "What's wrong with it; it looks lovely to me". He said, "Look at the pigment of my skin. I, by the accident of birth, am now discriminated against. The opportunities for progress in this world are denied me just because of the accident of birth, that I was born a colored man. Opportunities for advancement in every field, neighborhoods that I would like to live in and raise a family I couldn't move in, where I would like to open up a business I couldn't move into that area."

Then I told him my own personal experience, that I came to this country. Well, I didn't have that problem but I was a foreigner in the midst of all Americans. I didn't find it difficult.

"Yet", as he reminded me, "but that's not my problem, Neville. Others have come here speaking with an accent, but they haven't my skin, and I was born an American" . Then I told him an experience of mine in New York City. If I were called upon to name a man that I would consider my teacher, I would name Abdullah. I studied with that gentleman for five years. He had the same color skin, the same pigment as this gentleman. He would never allow anyone to refer to him as a colored man. He was very proud of being a negro didn't want any modification of what God had made him. He turned to me and he said, "Have you ever seen a picture of the Sphinx?" I said, "Yes". He said, "It embodies the four fixed quarters of the universe. You have the lion, the eagle the bull and man. And here is man that is the head. The crown of that creature called the Sphinx, which still defies man's knowledge to unriddle it, was crowned with a human head. And look carefully at the head, Neville, and you will see whoever modeled that head must have been a negro. Whoever modeled it had the face of a negro and if that still defies man's ability to unravel it, I am very proud that I am a negro." I have seen scientists, doctors, lawyers, bankers, from every walk of life seek an audience with old Abdullah, and everyone Who came thought themselves honored to be admitted to his home and to receive an interview. If he was ever invited out, and he was, he was always the honored guest. He said, "Neville, you must first start with self. Find self, don't be ashamed ever of the being you are. Discover it and start the changing of that self".

Well, I told this gentleman exactly what Abdullah had taught me, that there was no cause outside of the arrangement of his own mind. If he was discriminated against, it was not because of the pigment of his skin, though he showed me signs as large as all outdoors denying him access to a certain area. The sign is there only because in the minds of some men such patterns are formed and they draw unto themselves what now they would condemn; that there is no power outside the mind of man to do anything to man, and he by the arrangement of his own mind, by consenting to these restrictions in his cradle and being conditioned slowly through his youth, waking into manhood believing himself set upon would have to be set upon, but "no man cometh unto me save I call him". So then someone comes to condemn or to praise. They couldn't come unless I call them. Not a man called Neville, but that secret being that is not called Neville. The secret being that is the sum total of all of my beliefs , all of the things that I consent to, that form a pattern ofstructure, that secret being draws unto itself things in harmony with itself. Well, that man went away and wrestled with himself. He couldn't believe everything I told him, not that night, but last Sunday morning in the lobby, he came forward and we renewed the friendship. He took me next door to show me the fruit of this teaching .

He said, "Neville, it took me almost three years to really overcome that fixed idea that I, by the accident of birth, would be a secondary citizen, but I overcame .it. Now here is my office on Wilshire Boulevard. I picked this one not because it was the only one offered; four equally wonderful spots were offered me. I took this one because it had greater telephone facilities , but the others were equally good.

Now here is my office. Now you couldn't judge my income from this office, lovely as it is. Everything is nice about it, but, Neville, this year I will net a quarter of a million dollars". Well in America that is still a fabulous sum of money. It would be staggering in any other part of the world, but even in fabulous America a man to net a quarter of a million is really up in the very highest of brackets. And that was the man that a few years ago told me the whole vast world was against him by reason of the accident of birth. He knows now he is what he is by virtue of the state of consciousness with which he is identified, and the choice is his to go back to the restrictions of his childhood when he believed the story or to continue in the freedom that he has found.

So you and I can be anything in this world we desire to be if we will clearly define our aim in life and constantly occupy that aim. It must be habitual. The concept we hold of self that is noble must not be put on just for a moment and taken off when we leave this church. We feel free here; we feel that we have something in common, that's why we are here, but are we going to wear the noble concept we now hold of self when we go through the door and enter that bus, or are we going to return to the restrictions that were ours prior to coming here? The choice is ours and the hardest lesson to learn is that there is no one in this world that can be drawn into your world unless you, and you alone, call him.

So do not do what they did thousands of years ago, for that is the beginning of the secession of the great truth.

So we are told they turned away from it, never again to walk with it, and the few who remained didn't like it either, but where would they go if this is the word of eternal truth? Not that it's true for this day and age, but if this is the law of being, and in all the dimensions of my being it holds good, if this is eternally true, then let me learn the lesson now, though I wrestle with myself as he did for three years.

So, the changing of the feeling of "I" is a selective thing because unnumbered states are infinite states, but the "I" is not the state. The "I" believes itself to be the state when it enters and fuses with it, so he was presented with a state and without the faculty of discrimination in his youth, he fused with the state and believed these restrictions were true, and it took him three years to disentangle the "I" from these fixed ideas with which he had lived for so many years. Now you may take only a moment or you, too, may take your three years. I can't tell you how long it's going to take you but I'll tell you this much. It can be measured by the feeling of naturalness. You can wear a feeling until it's natural. The moment the feeling becomes natural, it will begin to bear fruit within your world.

So I told this story at a small gathering here in the city, and not very many asked questions about it, but three people asked, "But he must have had money before. He must have known the right people. He must in some way have had some substance to start it, because how can you go out to loan a hundred million dollars and call that a real fact of being that you have that to loan and tell me you didn't have some one who had it or you, yourself, didn't have it".

I did not ask the gentleman about the individual facts of the case. I went into the office, I saw it, I didn't look at his books; he volunteered this information, and gave me the figure of a quarter of a million net for the year. I have not checked or in any way verified the statement; I believe it implicitly. But I will not go along with those who believe that unless you have certain things to start with you can't apply this law.

You can start now from scratch and choose the being you want to be. You aren't going to change the pigment of your skin but you will find your accent or the pigment of skin or your so-called racial background will not be a hindrance, for if a man is ever hindered it can only be the state of consciousness in which he abides that hinders him. Man is freed or constrained by reason of the state of mind in which he persists. If you persist in it, well, then I will say, "persist in it", but I warn you no one cares and that is an awful blow when a man discovers that no one, no one but himself really cares. So we find ourselves weeping with ourselves in the hope of getting others to weep with us. And what an awful shock when the day arrives we discover that no one really ever cared. They will give us some little listening ear for a moment just as they were passing by, but they really didn't care.

When we make that discovery we shake ourselves out of it and boldly appropriate the gift our Father gave us before that the world was. So let me show you the gift. You've read your Lord's Prayer possibly daily, but you read it as a prayer from a translation of a translation which does not reveal the sense of the evangelist.

The real translation, you will find in Farrar Fenton's work where in the original it is written in the imperative passive mood, which is like a standing order, a thing to be done absolutely and continuously. So that you can look now upon your universe as one vast inter-knit machinery where all things happen.

There isn't a thing to become; all things are taking place, so it is written in this manner, "Thy will must be being done. Thy kingdom must be being restored." It is the only way you could express it if you would express the imperative passive mood. But from the Latin from which our translation was made there is no first aorist of the imperative passive mood. So we have it in the way we have it but it does not reveal the intent of the mysteries. If you will see all things are now, you don't become, you simply select the state that you would occupy. Occupying it you seem to become but it is already a fact, every aspect of that state in its most minute detail. It's worked out and taking place. You by occupying the state seem to go through the action of unfolding that state, but the state is completely finished and taking place. So now you can choose the being you want to be and by choosing a being other than what you are now expressing you start the change of the feeling of "I".

Now, how will I know that I have changed the feeling of "I"? By beginning first with an uncritical observation of my reactions to life and then noticing my reactions when I think I am identified with my choice. If I assume that I am the man that I want to be, let me observe my reactions.

If they are as they were, I have not identified myself with my choice, for my reactions are automatic and so if I am changed I would automatically change my reactions to life. So the changing of the feeling of "I" results in a change of reaction, which change of reaction is a change of environment and behavior. But let me warn you now. A little alteration of mood is not a transformation; it's not a real change of consciousness. Because as I change my mood for the moment it can quickly and rapidly be I would say, replaced by another mood in the reverse direction. When I say that I was changed, as that gentleman changed his mood, his basic mood, his state of consciousness, it means that having assumed that I am what the moment denied, what my reason denied, that I remain in that state long enough to make that state stable. So that all of my energies are flowing from that state. I am no longer thinking of that state. I am thinking from that state. So that wherever a state grows so stable as to definitely expel all of its rivals, then that central, habitual state of consciousness from which I think defines my character and is really a true transformation or change of consciousness. Whenever I reach that state of stability, watch my world mold itself then in harmony with this inner change. And men will come into my world, people will come to aid and they will think they are initiating the urge to help. They are playing only their part. They must do what they do because I have done what I did. Having moved from one state into the other. I have altered my relationship relative to the world round about, and that changed relationship compels a change in behavior relative to my world. So they have to act differently toward me.

So in changing the "I", you start with desire, which we will unfold and elaborate on tomorrow night. For it starts with desire. Desire is the spring of action, for you must want to be other than what you are. We fail because we do not fall in love enough with an idea. We aren't, I would say, moved enough to want to be other than what we are. If I could get you to be completely in love with some state to the point where it haunted the mind, I could almost prophesy that you would in the not distant future externalize that state within your world. And the reason we fail we aren't hungry enough to change. For either we do not know the law or we haven't the urge or the hunger to really bring about the change.

For the changing of the feeling of "I" results in the change of reaction, which change of reaction results in a change of world. If you like your world and you are complacent about it, you haven't started on the road of the mysteries, for the very first beatitude appeals to one who is not complacent. "Blessed are the poor in spirit". You must be poor in spirit, not complacent, not satisfied. The man who thinks that by reason of birth, the religion that he inherited at birth, is good enough for me, that he is not dissatisfied, he is not, I would say moved that being is complacent and therefore he is not poor in spirit; he is very rich in spirit. Theirs is not the kingdom of God. For if I could stir you, make you dissatisfied with self, then you will recognize that self and set about to change it. For the only field of activity for man is within himself and on himself. You do not work on the other. The day you change self, that day you change your world.

Now I see my time is going to its quick end. And so in the remaining minute I have left here let me not urge you, because if you come to the meeting tomorrow night not really hungry, you wouldn't benefit, but I do hope that many of you are there. Even if you are stirred to the point of trying to, I would say, disprove what I told you, I would accept that challenge for in the attempt to disprove it, I know if you were sincere in your attempt, you would prove it. So I hope many of you will come and take this feast with us. We are here in the city at the Ebell for 15 nights, Monday thru Friday, as Mr. Smith told you, for three consecutive weeks. If you can't take all, and I do hope many of you will take all, then pick out the title s that appeal to you. Tomorrow night to me is basic; it is the importance of defining an aim in this world, having a goal, for without an aim you are aimless. And you were warned in the Book, or I would say, in the Epistle of James that "the double minded man is unstable in all his ways. Let not such a man believe that he shall receive anything of the Lord; for he is like a wave that is driven and tossed by the wind." That man never reaches his goal. So you must have an aim, and tomorrow night we will show you the importance of defining desire. There are certain schools who teach you to kill out desire; we teach you to intensify desire and show you the reason for such teaching, show you what the Bible teaches about desire.

And now we will come to the help that many of you have asked for today. Those who were not here on Sunday let me remind you it is a very simple technique. As I told you on Sunday, any time that you exercise your imagination, and do it lovingly on behalf of another, you are mediating God to man. So we sit quietly and we simply become imitators of our Father. And He called the world into being by being the thing he would call. And so we sit and we listen as though we heard someone congratulating us on having found what we seek. So we go to the end of the matter and we listen just as though we heard, and we look as though we saw, and we try in this manner to feel ourselves right into the situation of our answered prayer, and there we wait in the silence just for about two minutes, and so they will lower the lights to aid you. And let me remind you if you want to clear your throat, please do so. If you want to shift your position in the chair, do so. Feel as though you are alone at home, because if you don't and you try not to disturb the neighbor, you will not be able to exercise your imagination on behalf of anyone. So now I will take the chair and just simply listen attentively, just as though you heard. I'll make you this promise - the day you are very still in mind and really become attentive, you will hear as coming from without what really you are whispering from within yourself.

LESSONS FROM THE LECTURE

1. CONSCIOUSNESS SHAPES REALITY:
Neville emphasizes that the external world is a manifestation of one's consciousness. Your environment and circumstances are a reflection of your inner state of mind.

2. CHANGE FROM WITHIN:
To alter your external circumstances, you must first change your inner thoughts and beliefs. Attempting to change the outer world without changing your mind is futile.

3. IDENTITY VS. STATE:
Neville distinguishes between your individual identity (the "I" or imagination) and the state you occupy. You can choose the state with which you identify, and this choice is crucial.

4. ACCEPTANCE OF SELF:
Self-acceptance is the cornerstone of personal transformation. To change, you must first acknowledge and accept your current self, no matter how unappealing it may seem.

5. RESPONSIBILITY FOR YOUR LIFE:
Neville teaches that you are the sole architect of your fortunes and misfortunes. Blaming others for your circumstances is counterproductive. Take responsibility for your life.

6. START WITH SELF-OBSERVATION:
Begin the transformation process by critically observing your reactions to life. Recognize your automatic responses and beliefs.

7. DESIRE AS A CATALYST:
Desire is the driving force behind change. You must have a deep and passionate desire to be different from your current self to initiate transformation.

8. PERSISTENCE AND STABILITY:
Real change comes when you persist in a new state of consciousness until it becomes stable. Your inner transformation should be so profound that it changes your reactions and behaviors consistently.

9. NO EXTERNAL LIMITATIONS:
External factors like race or background should not hinder your transformation. Neville believes that a change in your state of consciousness can overcome any external limitations.

10. MEDITATION AND IMAGINATION:
Neville introduces a technique involving imagination and meditation. By imagining your desires as fulfilled and listening attentively, you can bridge the gap between your current state and your desired state.

SOUND INVESTMENTS

Neville Goddard 1953

Today's subject is "Sound Investments".

I want to share with you today what I consider one of
the truly great revelations of all time.

On Sunday morning, April 12th, my wife woke from
what was really a deep, profound sleep and as she was
waking a voice distinctly spoke to her; and the voice
spoke to her; and the voice spoke with great authority
and it said to her: "You must stop spending your
thoughts, your time and your money; everything in life
must be an investment." So she quickly wrote it down
and went straight to the dictionary to look up the two
important words in the sentence, 'spending' and
'investing': the dictionary defines 'spending' as "to
waste, to squander, to layout without return." To
'invest' is to "layout for a purpose, for which a profit is
expected" .

Then I began to analyze the sentence - "You must stop
spending your thoughts, your time and your money,
for everything in life must be an investment". As I
dwelt upon it, I saw where everything is NOW; that
through the portals of the present all time must pass,
and this psychological NOW, the state in which I find
myself now, does not recede into the past. It advances
into my future.

So, what I do NOW is the all important thing, and
thought is the coin of heaven; it is the money of
heaven; and so the thought I entertain now, the
thought to which I consent, as told us in Ephesians "All
things when they are admitted are made manifest by
the light, and all things when they are manifested are
light:" and the word 'light' is defined as consciousness.

So the state to which I now consent must be made manifest, and when it is manifest, it is only that state of consciousness made visible, coming to bear witness of the state in which I abided.

So, every moment of time, I am either spending or I am investing. Unfortunately most of us spend the coin of heaven, and morning, noon and night we live in negative states for which there is no return, when we could easily have spent, not spent, but invested that moment, so at the end of that day we really would have a wonderful portfolio. The religious minded person invests possibly on Sunday morning. Through the service he is lifted for a moment; if he is not overly critical he might be carried away with the hymn; he might be carried away with the solo, the organ music, the address from the pulpit, and for a moment he is investing; but the rest of the week he spends.

Now you know from experience if you put all your money into one great concern, it may be wonderful, it may be sound, but at the end of a year the directors may decide to reorganize and therefore decide to pass the dividend, and if you depended on a dividend check for your daily needs, though it is a good, firm, wonderful concern, when they passed the dividend, then you must either sell some stock or raise or borrow on it. While every moment of time you could have a most marvelous portfolio and if one passes a dividend check it does not matter. If you devoted every moment of time to positive thinking, constructive thinking, by not accepting any rumour that does not contribute to the fulfillment of your desire, no matter what it is - it could be the most obvious fact in the world - if it does not contribute to the fulfillment of your dreams, do not accept it.

If you do you are spending; if, not by denying, but by complete indifference, complete non-acceptance, you turn to what you wish you could have heard instead of what you heard, you are investing. It's not the hearing that matters, its the admitting the truth of it that matters.

All things when they are admitted, not all things when they are heard, but if you give consent to it, if you accept it as true; then you either spend by acceptance or you invest depending on the nature of the state accepted. So, this revelation which came through my wife to me is one of the greatest that I have heard; had it been told in our Bible, it would have been told in its strange meter "And the Lord God spoke unto her this day and said to her, his servant" and they would have told what revelation would have come in that manner but it came to a normal natural wife, came in a normal natural manner to instruct not only her, but to instruct her husband, for I was the first one to whom she told it and I can't tell you what it has done to me since I heard it on the morning of the 12th April, for it made me more aware of the moment, made me far more conscious of every moment of the day so that I am not spending; I must invest - time is too precious and because these moments do not recede. they do not pass away; they are always advancing into my future to either confront me with a waste or to show me some wonderful return; if I invest it's for a purpose and, therefore, I hope, not only hope, I expect a reward: I expect a profit on my investment. So a moment spent now, this very day, could tomorrow pay you great dividends.

Now I told a story here two weeks ago of Jimmie Fuller. Well, I didn't have all the details of the story, but after the meeting; dozens of you said to me, not only after the meeting that day, but after my meetings at the Ebell Theatre, that Jimmie Fuller to have made the fortune that he made, must have had great capital. Well, I could neither affirm nor deny your bold assertion, for you spoke as though you knew and many of you almost convinced me that he had great capital and that's why he turned it into great returns. So on Friday night I asked him to tell me more of the details. He said "When you came here four years ago, Neville, I came to hear you. My wife asked me 'Why do you come to hear Neville? Who told you of Neville? He said, I turned the radio on one night and I heard Dr. Bailes. I had never heard of the man before. At the end of his lecture, which I thoroughly enjoyed, he said Neville is coming to speak for us and it's a MUST. Well the next night, I so liked Dr. Bailes that I turned him on the next night, and for the next two weeks he kept on promoting you, and he was so generous in his praise, I thought I've got to hear this man. So when I came, I enjoyed what I heard on Sunday morning, and then you announced you were speaking the following night at this place, but it was two dollars. Well, he said, between myself and the next I actually had Fifty four dollars. I had a wife and a little boy; we couldn't leave the little child alone; he was a babe: it meant a sitter-in, but my wife and I came to everything you gave and one night we could not pay the sitter-in; we just didn't have it, but we took our last which was fifty four dollars and came to your every meeting - the two of us - and one night we didn't have it to pay that sitter-in. Three years later, Neville, I had not proven your theory. You know my problem, as I told you before."

Perchance there is someone here who did not hear it - the man is a negro, and his problem was that because he was a negro, all the marks and stripes of the world were against him. I tried to convince him it was only in his own mind that these stripes were placed; his acceptance of that as restriction made it restriction, but if he could only drop it by non-acceptance, by complete indifference, to the pigment of skin he could accomplish his every dream by acceptance of it now.

Well, in the last year, Jimmie Fuller by complete acceptance, investing his moment, his now, has turned the year into a net profit of two hundred and fifty thousand dollars. He did not have one penny when he started; he did not raise large capital; he didn't have it. He only invested God's coin. God gave it to him. He gave him the moment, which is time. So instead of spending his thought, which everyone has, and spending his time. which everyone has, he had no money, but he knew that thought was money; so he invested his thought in the now, knowing that it was not going to recede and vanish from sight; that was an investment: it would advance into his future.

Well it did. It so advanced that he tells me now everything he touches turns to gold. Now he has three children; they come here every Sunday to Sunday school: he doesn't want his children to start with his stripes, so he wants them to feel what this Church gives. So every Sunday, Jimmie tells me many a Sunday he feels like taking off for the beach or up to the mountains with his wife, but he will not go because he wants his children to have an opportunity he didn't have. He says "My people were very religious, but they must have worshipped a very poor God, for they were steeped in poverty.

So I just wouldn't go near the churches of my mother and my brothers and these people, because I couldn't conceive of such a God doing that to us; yet they never missed service. For when I found in this what I found here in this Science of Mind Church, I brought my children to Sunday School. Now this is what happened to them. Here God is love, and love surrounds them and they know nothing but love, that God is love. For one day my little girl which is the youngest of the three, was quite sick, a beastly cold. and that night when the little boys said their prayers. these are the words they used 'Thank you God, that sister is perfect tomorrow.' They could not look at the little girl, sick as she was, and say 'Thank you God that sister is well now', but they said 'Thank you, God, that sister is perfect tomorrow'. Neville, it was a miracle. The next day that child was perfect; there wasn't the sign of a cold - a complete absence of all that we saw the night before, and these two little brothers simply gave thanks."

"Now, he wanted a watch. I wouldn't give him the watch. I could have bought a thousand watches for him. I want my little son to learn a law which I didn't know until recently. So he filled his mind with the possession of a watch, and he spoke of the watch as a 'live' watch - one that ticks, one that is alive, not a toy watch. So then he fills his mind with the possession of the watch. On his way to school he found a 'live' watch. Now he knows the working of law - that the complete acceptance of the state in consciousness must result in an externalization of the state accepted. So if he accepts the watch he need not turn to his earthly father, as the medium through which the watch will come. I don't want to think for one second he has to point to his mother or his father as the only channels through which his good will come.

I want him to recognize an Infinite Father - the Father of US all - who gave to him as he gave to me everything that I will accept. I want my children to learn it as I have learned. Yes, I could shower him with gifts, but then he would look to me as the only channel through which it will come. That I must not accept. So you should see the little boys and little girls actually live by this law. God to them is love and the only reality and love surrounds them. So they never miss the Sunday School here."

Then he goes on to tell me all other wonderful things that have happened by the mere acceptance of this law. He said. "The getting of my car, this convertible Cadillac - I treated it loosely, I sat quietly in my living room and drove my Cadillac, and I simply treated for this loosely," he said, "I didn't put real effort into it, I accepted it and then when I decided to get it I simply put in three telephone calls and that day I was driving this car, Neville. Now everything happens just like that. Today, instead of going to my office and working in the office I work behind the scenes. I sit all day and I hear the report that is good from my employees; my entire office staff must tell me good news, the only thing I will allow myself to hear. I ride my car; I'm in the office; I am at home; I'm in the office but I am only hearing good news, and seldom do I go to the office physically to do office work, so I am behind the scenes only hearing good news. So I have completely forgotten the so-called pigment of skin and, Neville, honestly I can tell you today I feel that I am blessed beyond all men because I was born a negro. I am so proud to be born a negro; I am so proud I'm one."

And here is a story that will interest all of you; he said "I had some property to dispose of, I had certain things in investments for those who had money, and so I advertised it and a man called me on the wire. He saw the ad, and asked me if I was the gentlemen, so I told him I was the one who had the property. The first thing he said to me, "I don't want any nigger property." Jimmie said, "I didn't answer, as if I hadn't even heard the word. If he wants to be prejudiced, he may be prejudiced, that's his right. He wants to be silly about it, that's his right. He can spend; he need not invest. So I said, "It is perfectly all right, sir, I have all kinds of property, I have all kinds of things for your investment." A week later he called me up and said, "Would you come and see me." He said, "I went to see him. When I got out of my car his knees almost buckled, for he didn't know a negro was coming to see him, and a negro walked up his stairs into his living room." He said within a matter of minutes he purchased $37,000 worth of mine that I had to offer. He said the first $25,000 that he bought he simply bought that to buy back his face, and then the remaining $12,000 he bought that because it was a very good investment. Well, since that time this gentleman has spent tens of thousands of dollars with me and constantly calls me to thank me because they are such wonderful investments.

Now here is a man who is proud of his skin; he has no prejudices because that's spending his time, he can't afford to spend. So in harmony with the revelation given to my wife, let us all now stop spending our thoughts, our time and our money. For everything in our life must be an investment. We know the truth. This platform radiates the truth.

You are told that everything proceeds out of your own consciousness, but what you and you alone accept as true, that will externalize itself and mold itself in your environment. All the conditions that you will encounter will simply bear witness of the state you have accepted. Well, if you don't like what you are encountering, then stop spending and learn the art of investment for every moment of time is an opportunity to invest, not to spend; yet on the other hand, you and I are free, we are free to waste every coin in the world. For that we have a right, we are free beings, we can spend, we need not invest, but if you know you can invest, why not choose the wiser way.

Now we are told in the thirtieth chapter of the Book of Deuteronomy, "The commandment I command you this day is not hidden, and it isn't far off. It's near unto thee; it is in thy mouth and in thy heart. Now, I set before you this day, life and good, death and evil, blessings and cursings. Choose life, choose blessing." But the choice is ours for we are free. He sets before us this day, this very moment, a commandment. He sets everything before us; it's not far away, it's in our tongue right now. And before me now is a blessing or a curse; I can accept the fact you don't like me; it doesn't matter, you may love me; but if I accept the fact that you don't like me, don't like the teaching, I'm spending my time. Tomorrow you'll prove to me that I have spent my time by your behavior relative to me. On the other hand, if I accept the fact that you do like it, because you are proving it, then I would have no doubt in my mind that you could not do anything other than contribute to this teaching. So it is up to me to either bless myself or curse myself.

I can choose life or I can choose death. I can choose the good, but I am free, I can choose the evil.

It's entirely up to me. But if you and I loved this, accept it and believe it, then we are wise indeed if, knowing the whole is before us, we go out determined to become investors, not spenders, not wasting and squandering our substance, but laying it out for a purpose. Every moment become conscious of the moment, what are you doing. I am accepting now the fact that I am a noble, dignified, wonderful being, that my father is proud of the son who is like him. So I will not hear or accept as true anything other than that which contributes to that noble concept I will hold of myself. For I will see that I am secure, and maybe a headline would startle the world but I will not accept it, for if I don't admit to it, it can't proceed out of me. For all things when they are admitted are made manifest, not unless they are admitted.

So if I now will admit that using this moment as my moment to invest, if I am what reason denies, what my senses deny, and I proceed in that assumption, knowing that even though it doesn't confirm itself tonight or tomorrow, I will still live in the assumption that I am what I want to be and all day tune in and listen only for the good report. I know these are investments and tomorrow these dividend checks must come. They must come. That's the law of our being. So everyone here, take it to heart, and though you don't need money, and so I say to the hundreds of you who say to me in private, "He must have had money", I tell you I know the story now; I didn't know it when you boldly claimed that he had money but now I have it from the source. He only had $54.00 and the $54.00 he spent coming to my meetings, even when he couldn't spend a dollar on a sitter-in; so I tell you he didn't have it; he has it today. But you don't need even $54.00.

All you need is time and you have it, it's now. All you need is the thought, that's money. So instead of spending that now, and spending the thought in the now, invest it now, for your now, this very moment as I stand here and I will get off the platform in a little while - and you will think, well now this is gone, he'll come back next year - this is not gone. What I am doing now is not going to slip away; it's going to move forward and embody itself as a condition, embody itself as the circumstance of my life. So that my now's, my reactions to what I am hearing and saying and seeing, all of my reactions are in the now, and my reactions are spelling out my tomorrow. So I will repeat it - through the doorway of now - because he said, "I am the door", I am is always first person present. Not I was the door, or I will be the door; "I am the door," "I am the resurrection," so what I do in the present, now, is not going to recede, it is going to advance into my future for through the door of the present, of the now, all time must pass. Now don't spend it as it passes; as it passes through the door of the now, invest it. Every moment of your life see that it is a positive, constructive, noble moment. I promise you a wonderful, healthy, radiant future if you will invest the now.

Now this being my last talk for a little while, I would like while I have this opportunity because the theatre, the Ebell, can't take all of you, I hope that many of you will come this coming week and make it a really fruitful, wonderful week, but I know you can't all get into the Ebell; so here, one lady as I came through the door said, "Neville, you made it so clear on Friday night; something I'd not seen before, for you told us this year you brought a wonderful revelation and that is the wide difference between thinking from an end and thinking of an end.

For you emphasized that time and time again since you've been here this time, but I didn't get it until Friday." I said, "Well, how did you get it?" She said, "Your picture of the balcony and the stage." Well, now we have the same situation here. We have a balcony, so we have a stage. Well, if she having heard it so often didn't get it, the chances are many of you didn't get it. Well, now she got it by my illustration, so I will repeat the illustration that all may get it. I said that when a man learns the art of thinking from the end, that man is master of his fate, for he defines his end, he formulates an aim in life, and then feels himself right into the situation of that end. So he thinks from it instead of thinking of it. The average man defines his dreams but he remains back here looking at them before he's thinking of them. The wise man occupies the state of his dreams, so he radiates from it, he thinks from it. And then to use this little illustration. I'm standing here looking out at the auditorium, and I would describe this theatre based from this angle, for I am seeing it from the stage. You, sitting in the auditorium, or sitting in the balcony, you are looking at it from that state, so you would see the screen and the speaker.

So the difference between us we see the same theatre from different angles. I would define it from here; you would define it from there. If I desired to get your point of view, while standing here I would assume that I am seated where you are and therefore within my imagination look from that position. I would then have to see the stage, not the auditorium; I would see the thing behind me, this cyclorama, and I would describe the theatre from that position which I am assuming that I am.

Now, if that position represents, say one of security and this one of insecurity I would then assume by physically standing here assume that I am now secure. And to prove that I am, I would then look from the state of security, so I would describe the world relative to my assumption. If I am still seeing what I saw when I was insecure, I have not succeeded in occupying that desirable end; I am still only thinking of it. So the wide difference between thinking from and thinking of must be clearly seen and then see the wisdom in learning the art of thinking from a desired end.

So here, look out at your world, formulate your lovely aims in life and just ask yourself, "What would it be like were it true that I now embody that state? How would I feel?" And in response to that question would come a feeling, a feeling that corresponds to that end. Learn then to think from that end, though reason denies it, though everything denies it, you occupy that end. It's now, you're investing it and these will become real within your world.

Now another thought that I tried to make clear and it's this which again Jimmie Fuller told me was one of the cues in his success. When the action of the inner man corresponds to the action the outer man must take in order to appease his desire, he will definitely realize his desire. There are two of us; there is an inner man and an outer man. The outer man is always made to say, "I of myself can do nothing; the Father within me, this inner one, He doeth the work. What I see him do, that, I, the outer do also." So there is an inner you.

If I now sat here and immobilized my body by relaxing it and then imagine what the outer would have to do in order to appease his desire, and with the outer relaxed, just let me imagine that I am actually it now, so I keep the body immobilized but I imagine that I am actually experiencing it now. I would experience in my imagination that which I would have to experience in the flesh to appease desire, and then imagine that state over and over and over, so that the actions of the inner man correspond to the actions the outer must take in order to realize desire. When that is done - I promise you it's going to be done in the flesh; no power in the world could stop it when these two actions coincide, but let it always be from the inner you.

And now at the end of the silence, this is what we do. Knowing that any time that we exercise our imagination lovingly on behalf of another, we are actually and literally mediating God to man. So we can sit quietly in the darkness and simply listen as though we heard the good report that we want to hear. We look into the darkness and imagine we are seeing what we want to see. This is then investing this two minutes; we have taken the moments that go to make up two minutes and really are investing it now. So when I take the chair and the lights are lowered let us listen and let us look as though we are hearing and seeing what we want to hear and see. And we are actually fulfilling the command of that wonderful voice that spoke to my wife when it said to her, "You must stop spending your time, your thought, and your money. For everything in life must be an investment." Let these two minutes be your greatest investment.

LESSONS FROM THE LECTURE

1. TRANSFORM YOUR THINKING:
The central message is to shift from a mindset of spending thoughts, time, and resources wastefully to one of investing them wisely. This transformation begins with changing the way you think about your thoughts and actions.

2. LIVE IN THE NOW:
Recognize the significance of the present moment (NOW). Understand that all time passes through this psychological NOW, and what you do and think in the present shapes your future.

3. THOUGHT IS CURRENCY:
View your thoughts as a form of currency. Just as money can be invested for profit, thoughts can be invested for positive outcomes. Guard your thoughts and make conscious choices about what you accept as true.

4. MANIFESTATION THROUGH ACCEPTANCE:
Understand that what you accept as true in your consciousness will manifest in your external reality. It's not merely hearing something but giving consent to it that matters. Be selective in your acceptance.

5. POSITIVE THINKING:
Embrace positive and constructive thinking. Refrain from accepting or entertaining thoughts that do not contribute to your desires. Instead, focus on thoughts that align with your goals.

6. INVEST IN EVERY MOMENT:
Realize that every moment presents an opportunity for investment. You can choose to invest in positive, noble, and constructive thoughts and actions, which will yield returns in the future.

7. SELF-CONCEPT MATTERS:
Your self-concept, the way you perceive yourself, is crucial. Invest in a positive self-concept by affirming your worthiness, nobility, and dignity. Believe in your own potential.

8. THINK FROM THE END:
Distinguish between thinking of a desired end and thinking from it. To manifest your desires, occupy the mental state of already having achieved them. Imagine and feel the desired outcome as if it were true now.

9. ALIGN INNER AND OUTER ACTIONS:
Recognize that there is an inner and an outer self. Ensure that the actions of your inner self align with the actions your outer self must take to realize your desires. Inner and outer harmony is key.

10. MEDITATE ON YOUR DESIRES:
Use the power of imagination to meditate on your desires. Visualize and emotionally engage with the state or outcome you wish to manifest. Consistently invest your thoughts in this inner experience.

INFINITE STATES

Neville Goddard | March 22, 1968

The following is a transcription of a lecture.

Quite often someone will say to me: "I don't think others understand you." I was asked this question: "When you use the word 'state' I don't think others know what you mean, so would you please explain it?" Tonight, I will try.

We are told: "You are sons of the Most High, all of you." (Not just a few, but all of us). "Nevertheless, you will die like men and fall".....into infinite states of consciousness, for states are that into which the sons of the Most High fall. A state is an attitude of mind, a state of experience with a body of beliefs which you live by. Always expressing a state, you identify yourself with it by saying: "I am poor or I am rich. I am known or I am unknown. I am wanted or I am unwanted. " I could go on indefinitely, because there are infinite states into which an individual son of the Most High may fall.

Blake made this statement: "Eternity Exists and All things in Eternity Independent of Creation which was an act of Mercy. By this it may be seen that I do not consider either the Just or the Wicked to be in a Supreme State, but to be every one of them States of the Sleep which the Soul may fall into in its deadly dreams of Good and Evil. " When you find yourself in a state or see a seeming other in a state, do not condemn or praise it, for all states exist and no state is greater than another. Every state is an attitude, a state of experience with a body of beliefs that an individual son of the Most High occupies.

And if that an individual son of the Most High, then are we not brothers of the Highest Unity? And are we not also members of the ultimate body who is God the Father? So the states into which we fall cannot mar or in any way deter our immortal self who fell.

Your creative power did not willingly fall. It was your Father's will that you, his creative power, descend into and experience states. In the 8th chapter of Romans, Paul tells us: "He was made subject unto futility, not willingly, but by reason of the will of him who subjected him in hope." There is unity in God, yet God the Father is made up of gods, the sons. So God's creative power fell into division and passes through states which results in resurrection into unity.

As a son of the Most High you can, in the twinkle of an eye, move into any state, but the chances are you will not remain there, for a state is made up of a body of beliefs! If you spend the day thinking from a certain base, a certain body of beliefs, the chances are you will fall asleep that night in the same belief. Knowing you can move into another state, another body of beliefs, you may try to move, but you must persist in staying in the new state until it becomes natural.

There are unnumbered states and the occupant of one state is not better than the occupant of another, for each is a brother in the highest unity and all are one in the body of God the Father. But the state, the attitude of mind to which you most constantly return, constitutes your dwelling place. If you dwell in self-pity you will express the state, but by occupying that state you are not less than one who has ambitions to enter the White House, or the Vatican as the Pope.

The individual desiring an ambitious state is not greater than or less than the one who doesn't know he is in a state and remains subjected to it.

How do you get out of a state? Through belief! You must believe in the doctrine. You are told: "Whatsoever you desire, believe you have received it and you will." The precepts of Christ must be accepted literally, for they will be fulfilled literally. Can you believe the precept that believing you have already received your desire will bring it forth in your world? If so, then tonight you can change the things that are happening in your world. And if you can believe and persuade yourself that things are as you want them to be to the point of actually moving into the feeling they are true, they will be felt and seen in your world. You must feel your desires are already realized, that they are already true, for the truth of any concept is known by the feeling of certainty that the thought is true.

Assuming you are not the man (or woman) you want to be, you will know that you are really it by the feeling of certainty it inspires in you, for if you feel certain, you will act upon it. If you don't act you are not convinced, for God in you is your own wonderful human imagination and God is always acting! You may be physically incapacitated, but you are forever acting in your imagination, who is God, the Father of your life.

By states I mean attitudes of mind. The New Testament begins: "The time is fulfilled and the kingdom of heaven is at hand; repent and believe the gospel." The word "repent" means "a radical change of attitude. " Your attitude need not be towards another, but an attitude regarding self.

If you feel you have nothing to live for you must repent by changing your attitude radically from that state. Don't condemn yourself for the state into which you have fallen. If you don't like it move into another. Don't feel sorry for yourself, for if you do you will make the state a habit and remain there for the rest of your days on earth. Instead, you can believe this doctrine and move out of any state.

Let me illustrate with this story. A gentleman, who attends the lectures, and his wife moved into their new home at the beach. Wanting some landscaping done, they invited five landscape artists to give them bids. Two wouldn't even bid because of the location of the property but after choosing one, the lawns and gardens as well as several trees were planted. Within six months three trees had died. Now, instead of getting angry and calling the man, demanding the trees be replaced, my friend decided to test his imagination; so while sitting in his car he imagined that he was leaning against the one healthy tree while gazing at the three which had appeared to be dead, but were now healthy and beautiful. Then one day the landscape artist came to the house, inquiring about the garden, especially the trees. It seems his men had used too much nitrogen in the fertilizer, which caused the roots to burn. Upon seeing the trees, he returned the following Tuesday and replaced them free of charge.

This same gentleman shared another experience with me, saying: "On my way to work the other morning I passed a very prominent building and said to myself, 'I wonder what it would be like to work there?' Knowing nothing about the company, I played with the idea of them offering me a fantastic salary and even imagined seeing my name on the office door.

That very day while at work I received a call from an agency hired to fill the executive positions for the company whose building I had passed, and whose employment I had just imagined. The agency was calling to ask if I would consider working for their client. I was so shocked to realize that the law could work so quickly, but now I know it does!"

You don't have to remain in a state if you have made a mistake. You can change states morning, noon, and night, but the state to which you most constantly return constitutes your dwelling place. It is from there you are going to live and perpetuate until you move in thought. As Blake said: "The oak is cut down by the ax and the lamb is slain by the knife, but their eternal form remains forever and reproduces its external form by the seed of contemplative thought."

The being that you really are descended to the weakness of the flesh, causing you to experience the state you are now in. Contemplate another state, and the same being who brought your present form into being will restore and make alive the other state, the state desired. This he will continue to do until his purpose is fulfilled. That purpose is to follow a certain pattern back into the unity of being. You see, in the beginning we were drafted. We did not volunteer to fall into these states. We were made subject into futility, not willingly but by the will of him who sent us. But when we return we will discover that we are the very being who subjected us. We are now the sons, destined to return as God the Father!

Now let me share with you a word that I use night after night. The word is "David" and means "lover; beloved ", but specifically "father's brother."

We are all brothers, yet after my resurrection and return into unity, David (father's brother) called me Father. The day will come when David will call you Father too, for he is [the] Father's brother. We are all brothers of the highest unity, predestined to resurrect into that unity which was broken in our fall into division. So David's name in the most specific sense is "uncle". If David is the father's brother and everyone is a brother in the fall into division, when resurrected into unity David is he who reveals everyone as the Father. Unity was broken for a purpose. God's creative might descended to experience states in order to become greater than it was prior to the descent. Having unity in thought, creative power fell into division and will be resurrected back into unity of thought once more.

So when I speak of states I am speaking of states of consciousness, attitudes of mind which create a body of belief. My sister and brothers at home do not believe in the same Christ as I do, even though we were all born in the same family and raised in the same environment. My brothers call themselves Christians but their definition of Christ would differ from mine. From their state of consciousness they believe in a man who lived two thousand years ago, yet I would tell you that Christ is God's creative power and wisdom which descends into states, resurrects, and returns as the being who sent it out. The day will come when you will understand all of these precepts as being literally true. Here is one to be found 1 John, the 3rd chapter, the 2nd verse: "We are now the children of God; it does not yet appear what we shall be, but we know that when he appears we shall be like him. " How will we know him? By becoming as he is!

The preachers of the world will tell you that when he comes, you will be like him in character, in your attitude towards life. You will be kind and considerate and have his fine qualities, but I tell you: you will be like him who is in the depths of your soul meditating you! This I know from experience.

It was in the year 1936 when I saw the rock that scripture claims as the God who gave me birth. One day while quietly sitting in the silence, a rock suddenly appears before my vision. Then it divides itself and just as quickly reassembles itself into a man seated in the lotus posture, meditating deeply. As I looked closer I discovered I was seeing myself meditating me! And then I knew that when he awoke I wouldn't vanish, but rather I would know that I am He! This thing called Neville who stands before you is his emanation. He brought it into being, and although you cut off its head a thousand times he will restore its eternal form by the seed of contemplative thought.

Nothing ceases to be, because all things exist in eternity and can be brought into being by this meditative being, who looks just like you, only raised to the nth degree of majesty. You have never seen your face look so beautiful. You have never seen it contain such majestic power, such strength of character. Looking at himself and knowing there is no other, as he glows like the sun you return to the being he is meditating in this world of mortality. When you have this experience you will have nothing to do with anyone who claims he or she is Christ. You will let no one deter you, for when you see him you will be just like him. Have you ever seen anyone in this world who is exactly like you?

Your children may resemble you but if you put a picture of one of them beside yours, you would know they were pictures of different people, would you not? No one has the same fingerprints or the same odor as another. But when you meet the rock that begot you and the God who gave you birth, you will know him because you will be just like him.

When you see this being in the depth of your soul you are seeing the one who descended into these states, meditating himself. You are his emanation, his reflection playing the parts he dreams. And when he awakes from his descent and begins to ascend, you are He! No two seeds of contemplative thought in the depths of the soul are identical. We are all brothers, and having been subjected, when we return to unity we are God the Father. Now you see who the word "David" means – "the father's brother." God the Father is my brother, who one day will rise and, taking me back to the unity of being, he will call me Father. That is David! That is the play! That is the mystery of life!

Now to come back to the beginning. Everything is a state. You can be any man, any woman that you want to be when you understand the mystery of states. A state is simply an attitude of mind, a body of belief, a phase of experience. Now don't be like the moon — which changes from a quarter, to a half, to three quarters, to full — or the earth, which repeats itself over and over again season after season. Have you ever noticed that at certain times of the year, the same set of circumstances happen to you? Every year it is always very hot when it is time for your vacation or you are always broke around Christmas? Or that when you eat strawberries you always break out in a rash? All of these are patterns created in the world of states in which we all live.

There are infinite states and combinations of states into which God, your own wonderful human imagination, falls. Fortunately there is a limit, which comes when infinite mercy (who is within you) steps beyond and awakens himself; and as he does, you — the one he put through the torment — awaken, enhanced by the descent into these states. And as one you return, bringing your gifts which are the result of your experiences traveling through these states. You bring your talents, of which the greatest is the art of forgiveness, the ability to enter into and partake of the opposite. When you see someone in despair can you represent him to yourself as he would like to be seen? And can you persuade yourself that what you see is real? To the degree that you are self-persuaded, he will become that man. Then you will have conquered by forgiveness! You will have taken him out of one state and placed him in another.

Now, every act of kindness is a death in the divine image for in every act you sacrifice yourself. Making alive what you no longer want to see, you die to that and live in what you want to see, so every kindness to another is a death in the divine image. By representing others to myself and persuading myself that they are as I would like them to be, to the degree that I am self-persuaded they will become it; and as they do, I die to what I formerly made alive. I lived in what I thought them to be, and then I died to that thought. I did it deliberately, so I laid it down myself! I have the power to lay it down and the power to pick it up again. I purposely laid my life down to what I saw and lifted it up to what I wanted to see, thereby resurrecting another (who is myself) into a new state. How often must I do it? Seventy times seven — or as long as it takes me to convince myself that it is true.

When I lay down my life for another, he is my brother, for we have the same Father. As brothers we fall into states and resurrect ourselves into the unity of the Father!

So the greatest talent, the greatest challenge to overcome, is the art of forgiveness. By forgiveness I do not mean a verbal agreement, leaving the memory of what was forgiven. To completely forgive, I must completely forget the event. No matter what was said, if you forgive me you can't even remember what I did or said. Only willing to see what you want to see, if you persuade yourself that you are now what you want to be, you have forgotten what you were before. That's forgiveness.

True forgiveness is complete forgetfulness. Blake tells us: "The art of living is forgetting and forgiving." If you don't completely forgive you cannot forget, for to forgive is to change your attitude towards another, and as you change, you forget what they said or did, thereby no longer keeping them in the state that compels them to do what they did! While in a state, man must play the part the state dictates, and man must play every part. God in his infinite mercy has hidden from us the parts we have played, because the shock would be too great if we were to see the horrors that we have committed as we passed through all these states. You see, when you fall into a state you can't help but act from that premise, and you can fall into any state!

I am not telling you that one state is right and another wrong. I am simply asking you to judge all states with love. If you are ever in doubt, always do the loving thing.

Then you will know you are doing the right thing. If someone comes to you and tells you they want a job, don't ask him how he lost his previous job; simply hear him tell you he now has a wonderful job. Do that and you have taken him out of the state of unemployment and placed him in the state of the gainfully employed.

I urge you to use your own wonderful creative power and deliberately move into the state of your choice. Make it now by occupying the state long enough so that it feels natural. Haven't you had a suit of clothes that felt so new you were conscious of them every moment? I know when I bought my first suit, I walked down Fifth Avenue thinking everyone I passed knew my suit was new. People passing paid no attention to me, but I was so aware, so conscious of my new suit. That's exactly what happens when you move into a new state. If the state of affluence is new, you think everyone knows it, but no one knows or cares whether you are rich or poor, so walk in the state until it becomes natural. The moment the feeling is natural, wealth is yours!

I paid thirty dollars for my first suit. Today a suit will cost me $200.00; but regardless of the cost, when the suit is new, I am aware of it. But let me wear it long enough for it to feel natural and I will no longer be conscious of it. The same is true for a state. You may desire the state of fame. If you will think you are famous and remain conscious of the state long enough to make it natural, as the thoughts flow from you they become a natural part of your body of beliefs, and the world will proclaim your fame.

Now let us go into the silence.

LESSONS FROM THE LECTURE

1. STATES OF CONSCIOUSNESS:
Neville Goddard emphasizes that our lives are defined by the states of consciousness we occupy. States are mental attitudes, belief systems, and experiences that shape our reality.

2. UNITY AND BROTHERHOOD:
All individuals, as sons of the Most High, are interconnected and belong to the highest unity. Recognizing this unity helps in understanding the interconnectedness of all beings.

3. CREATIVE POWER AND PURPOSE:
It is our creative power and God's will that led us to descend into and experience various states. These experiences serve a purpose, leading us to greater growth and unity of thought.

4. CHANGING STATES:
You have the power to move into different states, but persistence in staying in a new state until it becomes natural is essential for achieving your desires and goals.

5. BELIEF AND MANIFESTATION:
Believing in the doctrine that "whatsoever you desire, believe you have received it and you will" is crucial for bringing your desires into reality. Your beliefs shape your experiences.

6. SELF-IDENTIFICATION:
How you identify yourself within a state matters. You can be anyone you desire, but you must assume and feel that identity as if it were already true.

7. FORGIVENESS AND TRANSFORMATION:
The art of forgiveness is the ability to completely forget and change your attitude towards others. This act of kindness allows individuals to shift from one state to another and helps in personal growth.

8. REPRESENTATION AND PERSUASION:
Representing others in a state they desire and persuading yourself that it is real can transform their reality. This concept underscores the power of the imagination and belief.

9. PATTERNS AND REPETITION:
Many life circumstances repeat themselves due to patterns created in the world of states. Recognizing these patterns and consciously shifting states can break the cycle.

10. NATURALIZATION OF STATES:
Just as a new suit feels noticeable at first but becomes natural with time, occupying a new state until it feels natural is key to manifesting desired outcomes.

THE COIN OF HEAVEN

Neville Goddard 1954

This being my last Sunday for a year, I wish to leave no doubt in your mind of what I tried to tell you in the last nineteen lectures. So I am going to ask a question which you can silently answer yourself. Have you lived this life of yours in such a way that you desire to live it again? Well, if you haven't, you'd better listen very carefully to what I will say this morning, if you have not already started, for may I tell you the next life is this life. When the eye is opened you will see it, that man unless he awakes and changes the tracks of this life he walks them forever. So if you have not lived this life in such a way that you really desire to live it again, you start now to interfere with these tracks and laying new tracks.

Let me give you just one simple little vision; these are all true visions of the speaker. Lying on my bed, suddenly the eye opened, the inner eye opened, and I saw a man casually dressed in working clothes walking the sidewalks of a major city. As he came to a hole that was open to receive coal, in fact the coal had just been delivered, he dropped something from his hand and bending down instead of picking up the thing dropped, he picked up huge hunks of coal that were scattered around the hole, and then my vision relaxed. When I re-concentrated the vision it was on the early part of that scene of the man walking down the sidewalk. He came to the manhole, he dropped, as he had in the previous state, bending down he picked up the coal as he had done before. Everything was in detail. As I saw it for the second time, I said "Now that scene hasn't changed one iota." My attention again relaxed; when I re-concentrated it, it was on the early part of the scene. Now

I could prophesy for that man; I knew exactly what he would do every moment of time right up to that manhole; that he would drop his package and not pick it up but pick up the coal. I knew he would look into that manhole and then change his mind either because someone below saw him pick it up and he didn't want the consequences of his action or else he had a change of heart, but I knew in detail what that man would do.

We are walking tracks and the tracks are forever, and by the mere curvature of time your next life is this life. You simply replay it: so if you have not so played it that you are proud of it, you start now and you start the change today.

We have given you a system by which you change it. For those who haven't heard why I say you walk tracks, you are standing forever in the presence of an infinite and eternal energy, and from this energy all things proceed, but they proceed according to pattern. Energy is moving in a certain pattern and you determine the pattern that it takes, for you actually lay down these tracks within you that energy flows over by the use of your inner conversations. This energy, I call it now mind, follows the tracks laid down in a man's own inner talking.

So if your inner conversations are not what they should be, I ask you today to start carrying on conversations within yourself from premises of fulfilled ideals; the man you want to be, the woman you want to be, if you have failed so far to embody it, now you begin to assume that you are that man, that you are that woman, and inwardly carry on conversations with your friends, those that respect you, or those you want to respect you, and carry on these conversations from the premises that they see in you the man and the woman that you want the world to see, just as though you were, and these words, inner words, which are really the breeding ground of future action will lay down new tracks and then the energy which is always flowing will flow over these tracks and the conditions and the circumstances of life will change. If you do not lay new tracks, I will prophesy for you you will find your self repeating it but you will not know you've done it before.

If I could only take you now into the inner vision with me and show you this room rising, everything rising in detail like a three dimensional curtain ascending, but everything is moving up and yet it remains. It is so altogether automatic that it ascends every moment of time the whole world is ascending, and as it ascends the world remains the same. It's almost as though not a thing has happened, and so you can't see it, but if the inner eye opens you see it ascend and as it leaves off that which begins is the duplicate, the perfect duplicate of the thing that rose and it rises in a three dimensional manner, so that when a man goes over these tracks he is totally unaware that he has walked them forever.

So I bring you a message to make you conscious: man must awake from the dream where he is simply an automaton. He moves like a machine, then he begins to awake and when he awakes then he is not that man at all that he seemingly in the past played for eternity. He awakes into a new being, a new man.

Now, the new man is a man of new conversations, as told you in Ephesians "Put off the former conversations, they belong to the old man that is corrupt, and put on the new man by a transformation of mind", and the new man is identified with completely new words. He speaks only the kind things; he is incapable of any unlovely thought in the world; he is incapable of even listening to the unlovely for inwardly he speaks only the kind, only the loving things of the world. Then he finds himself awakening a man within that was asleep; he awakens the second man which is called Christ Jesus in the Bible, which I tell you now is your own wonderful, loving imagination. When imagination awakes it is incapable of being exercised in any way outside of the loving way. So every time you use your imagination lovingly, you are literally awakening this inner man and you're mediating God to man. If I think of anyone in a loving way, I'm in contact with that being and God flows toward him.

Now because this is my last Sunday I will give you what I gave the class last Friday. Do not see it just as some metaphorical picture; see it as an actual picture. Imagine yourself at the very base of a wonderful waterfall and that water is flowing beautifully on you and imagine it's flowing through you and now from you and flowing towards someone you think of. I make this statement because it's a true statement; we are now in Eden but we are asleep as told you in the second of Genesis; man went sound asleep when he was placed to dress it and to keep it.

To awake, do this--just imagine yourself the center through which water radiates and everyone in this world is rooted in me and ends in me as I am rooted in and end in God: so I am in God's garden, it's Eden, but in God's garden every man in the world has a plot, a little garden. In that garden there are trees that grow, you can see them; if I look at this man now and inwardly look at his plot in my garden I will see the trees, some will be called health, some I call wealth, the tree of dignity, the tree of nobility, the tree of being wanted--they may be withered, they will never really die but they may be withered, they are in need of water. Just imagine that you are watering that plant and see in your mind's eye the leaves appear on what formerly was a barren plant. See the fruit appear and wherever he is in the world as you water his garden, which really is your own garden, as you water it he will embody the very qualities that the tree is now beginning to bear and radiate. You name the tree; whatever you name it, that it is: and you name this one if you know he is unwanted: he wants to be wanted. You name it and let the water flow towards it.

Imagine it's growing healthily in that garden and see it put out its leaves and see it put out its fruit. Wherever he is in the world he will begin to be wanted by people in his world. If he is unemployed, it's a tree of employment and see it radiate its leaves and radiate its fruit; he will be wanted and he will be gainfully employed.

I tell you this is not just an idle statement, everyone here can do it and everyone should do it, and when ever you water the tree in anyone's garden at the same time you are watering your own garden in the eternal one of God. For "I am the vine and ye are the branches", every man can say the same thing. So as you rise here, there are 2600 of you, you individually are the central vine of God's garden and everyone in your world is a branch in that vine. So when I, as a central vine, water a branch in my garden, at that same moment I am being watered and my garden is being watered in your wonderful garden. I don't have to water my own, just by taking care of the many gardens in God's Eden I take care of my own garden that is in the vine of everyone in the world.

You try it, and you can bless everyone in the world and then eventually the eye opens, the ear opens, the inner man awakes and you see the most glorious world which is always here to be seen, only we in our sleep had shut it out. We shut the whole wonderful golden world out by going to sleep and becoming an automaton; but take me seriously for your next life is this life.

You make this life what you want to make it because if you don't you will find yourself automatically and you won't even know it, because as a sleeping person you don't know you are walking the same track, but if I could only take you within me and let you see with the eye of the inner eye and watch these automatons in the world, sleeping people; yes, the eye is open and they seem to be awake, but they're really sound asleep for they're repeating the same thing.

Now become conscious; as you become conscious you enter the most glorious circle of awakened humanity. I call it the conscious circle of humanity, or as my old teacher used to call it "The Brothers". It simply means the awakened man and when he awakes they're all glorious beings for they are all the image of the Divine One. So try it, try it today with the art of revision. At the end of this day, review today. If some unlovely thing in the day, don't allow it, you rewrite it. Take that same scene and rewrite it, and having rewritten it replay it. In your imagination you imagine the action to be unfolding and you replay everything in the world; as you replay it as you ought to have played it the first time you've changed it. And the moment is never receding as people think, the moment is advancing.

Now this may seem an insane statement to tell you- - that yesterday is today's future: it seems insane you think it's not, it's past: but by the curvature of time you will discover but you will not know it, because you will be asleep unless you begin to awaken, and you will come upon what is yesteryear in your future, for the moment is never receding, it is always advancing into the future to confront us.

And so if you don't change it, you will simply find yourself repeating over and over what luckily in God's infinite mercy that sleep shuts out the memory of it, so you are doing it and you think you're doing it for the first time. But I ask you to awake for the purpose of this platform is to awaken everyone who comes here that we may all enter this brotherhood of awakened humanity.

Now we are told there were 'two gifts given to man at birth'--it doesn't mean this little birth when I left my mother's womb but when I left the womb of my Father that is the grand womb, the womb of creation when, before the world was, He created me and made me perfect and set me in this world for a purpose, educative purpose, but He gave me two gifts; He gave me His own mind and He gave me the gift of speech, the very thing He used to create a world. So He spoke the world into being and then gave me the gift by which he spoke the world into being; so He gave me mind and speech. If I use the gift wisely, and do it rightly, I will be led into the realization, into the fulfillment of my every desire; not one is beyond my ability to realize. If I continually use it wisely when I quit the body, as the world calls a man dead, when I leave this into another dimension by the wise use of the same two gifts, I will be brought into the company of the blessed, if I awake. If I don't use it wisely, I continue my circle of sleep; if I use it wisely, I will break the circle of recurrence and rise beyond it into eternity. If I don't, I continue on the curved line of time and repeat it over and over until some day I awake, for I am destined to be conformed to the image of His son.

So I have no doubt that everyone will awake but why not start the awakening process now? And you start it by practicing the art of revision. You try it; don't treat it idly. I ask you and I beg you to read and read over and over again the chapter "The Pruning Shears of Revision" and take it day after day, and never let the sun descend upon your wrath--any vexation, or any problem of the day. Resolve it before you sleep and carry that resolved picture into sleep and you will find the inner man awakening. But you try it with your friends and that you are the grand waterfall.

The Bible speaks of water, the mystic knows it does not mean water, it means truth, and so when I see anyone in my mind's eye and see him free, I am giving him the only truth that will set him free. So if I water his plant, imagine the water is really going to it and I see the leaves begin to appear and that man becoming free: he becomes healthy, he becomes secure, he becomes loved, then those trees are growing beautifully in my garden, and so as I do that, not only will he benefit from my watering his plant but I will benefit, I will begin to awaken.

So I ask everyone here to really try it. Now I know today the title was "The Coin of Heaven", but this being the last day, I thought I would simply give a sort of quick summary of what I have tried to tell you, for the purpose behind the nineteen lectures was to stimulate you to interfere with your time track that you may do something about it for the passage of time cannot change it. If you wait, thinking there is going to be some change beyond the grave, I tell you you will wait in vain.

There is no transforming power beyond the grave. All transforming power is in man now to interfere with his time track and you interfere with it by simply changing one moment in the course of a day, not accepting it as final no matter how factual the day. You know you did have that experience, don't allow the day to descend upon it and say "Well, I did have it". Go back to that moment in time. rewrite it, replay it in the revised version, and do it over and over in your imagination until that takes on the tones of reality. As it takes on the tones of reality you have changed your future. Take another incident and change it and keep on changing all the little episodes, all the little experiences and make them conform to a more idealistic experience and relive it.

If anyone is here for the first time, you might think, well that's fooling yourself, but you try it. Try it and see if the inner man will not awaken and when he awakens you will see a world that is automatic. You will see a world that's a machine and the whole vast world playing their parts that they've played forever, and will continue to play on the curvature of time forever until he snaps out of it and rises from the dead. As you are told, "Awake, you that sleep and rise from the dead."

The state called sleep now, is likened unto death where the son has died, so we are told the second son, the prodigal, that when he returned from that cycle and he was met, the father said: "He that was lost is found, and he that was dead is alive again".

So this state of lost-ness is likened unto death and the only purpose now is to rise; not to amass a fortune, although you are entitled to it, not to become famous, although you are entitled to it, but simply to awake from the state of sleep. And I know of no other way to awaken a man unless I can show him how mechanical he is and if you will take and practice seriously the art of revision, the eye will open and you will have the experiences the speaker spoke of. You, too, lying on your bed will find the eye peering into a city that may be 2000 miles away and there you will see more clearly than I see you now and you will watch the tracks of a man, and then disinterest and all of a sudden you decide to once more to be interested and you don't have a memory image of the man, you see the whole thing all over again. You see the man walk the same sidewalk, he does everything he did a moment before. Then take it back again, that track is laid forever and he will walk it forever until he awakes.

So I ask everyone here to take me seriously. If this seems a bit too mystical for you, I don't apologize; it's the only thing I can give you, for as I begin to awake I've got to give you the food on which then my father feeds me. He feeds me on new ideas; he changes my values, he changes all my meanings in the world. I don't have the same meaning I had last year; I don't have the same values I had last year; for the motives I had last year might have been along a different line; but then all of a sudden things change and you can't place value where formerly you placed it. You can't place it on wealth, you can't place it on names, you can't place it on recognition. All your values change and then you begin to inwardly see a new wonderful world.

So I tell you this garden of which I speak is a true garden, this you call the world. Don't believe for one moment you are in exile; this wonderful visible objective world of ours is not a place of exile, it's the living garment of my father. It really is his living garment but it needs interpreters. Individual men come as they begin to awaken and they will interpret for you this strange discordant harmony, for to you if I tell you, everything in your world is related by affinity to your own mental activity, you can't see it and so you can't quite see this discord as related to you if you didn't think that way that you know of, you weren't conscious of it. If you were conscious of the activity within you, you would see everything related to yourself, your own being. What you do not now see you will still know it is still related, so interpreters come because the interpreter as he begins to awaken, he knows this wonderful world has a voice for him that speaks of things behind the veil, behind the veil of your own mind, for behind your face right now there's an activity, an activity of your own imagination, and that activity, could you see it you would see it projected as the conditions and circumstances of your life. Not one thing is out of order, change the activity and you change the world in which you live, and you change that activity by the changing of your inner speech, for speech mirrors your mind and your mind mirrors God. If you don't change the speech you haven't changed the activity, and if you don't change the activity you can't change the conditions of life, for they only come bearing witness of this inner action of your mind.

So you want to change--I hope you do; but if you can now reflect upon your life, be it ten years, or be it sixty years, and you can't say within yourself "I would want to live this again if I had the freedom of choice", then you better start right now changing it, because I make you a prophesy, I make you a promise, your next life is this life. So if you cannot now in reflection say "I desire to live it again", then start today to lay down new tracks because if you don't you're going to live it again, and living it again you won't even know you are living it again. It is so altogether automatic, it's so effortless as you walk the tracks, for you stand in the presence of energy and you can't stop walking; you've laid them and you will walk them, and the curvature of time will bring you back and back and back forever and forever until you break it and you begin to awaken and when you awaken you enter a circle of awakened humanity. And I'll tell you you know them more intimately than anyone you now know in the state of sleep. There is not a person on earth that you know as intimately as those who have awakened when you awake.

When you go into their presence and you mingle with them you become one. You do not lose your identity: in fact you tend ever toward greater and greater individualization. You never become absorbed and lose your identity, but as you awaken you awaken to the being that you always were but you had forgotten it and went sound asleep. There is a beauty in the inner man that the outer has never touched, never scarred, and so as you awaken and they will be there to meet you because they are awaiting eagerly for the breaking of the circle of recurrence. So you try it.

We have told you many things this year, many things that seemed too mystical, but I warned you, when I took it four Sundays ago, this year I would give you the end of a golden string and I called upon you to roll it into a ball, and if you did it would lead you in at heaven's gate built in Jerusalem's wall.

Well, I felt I have given you that string but I cannot roll it into a ball for you. I promise you I will water your garden but it won't awaken you, it will awaken you only to lovelier things in a way, but it will not really break the circle for you, so I offer you now this day again the end of the golden string but I call upon you to wind it and roll it into a ball by the daily application of the principle of revision, by daily watching your inner actions and see if they correspond to the actions you desire to perform in the outer world.

Watch your conversations carefully; are they from premises of fulfilled ideas? If they're not, go back and make them and make them actually correspond to the ideal you want to embody in this world. Start, that is winding it into a ball and it will lead you in at heaven's gate built in Jerusalem's wall. I have no doubt in my mind for I know from experience that's how I opened up that wall; I opened it up by application. So I warned you every time I have taken the platform that the knowledge you have now is of no avail unless it's applied. A little knowledge if carried out in action is more profitable than much knowledge which you neglect to carry out in action.

If you had all the knowledge in the world and you didn't put it into practice, you wouldn't awaken.

Now here this morning everyone has heard it; you take it today and start this day revising, and watch the circle begin to snap, watch the eye begin to open, and I tell you there isn't a gift on earth, there isn't a possession in the world that you would want more than the opening of the eye when the eye opens. That's why I say your values change, the meaning of life changes, for you wouldn't sell the eye that opens for all the wealth of the world; you wouldn't exchange it for any recognition in the world now conferred upon the so-called great. You see the so called great all equally sound asleep playing their parts walking curved lines, and then you snap it and move into a wonderful world of awakened humanity and there you see these glorified beings, but really glorified beings, who preceded you into the conscious circle of humanity.

And now my time is up.

LESSONS FROM THE LECTURE

1. LIVE A LIFE WORTH RELIVING:
Neville Goddard begins by asking a fundamental question: Have you lived your life in such a way that you would want to relive it? This sets the stage for the importance of making conscious choices and actions in our lives.

2. THE NEXT LIFE IS THIS LIFE:
Goddard stresses that our future lives are not separate from our current existence. Instead, they are a continuation of our current life. This underscores the significance of making positive changes now to shape our future experiences.

3. AWAKEN FROM AUTOMATON-LIKE LIVING:
Many people live life like automatons, repeating the same patterns and actions. Goddard urges us to awaken from this unconscious state and become aware of our choices and actions.

4. INNER CONVERSATIONS MATTER:
Our inner conversations, thoughts, and beliefs are crucial in determining the direction of our lives. Changing our inner dialogue to align with our desired outcomes can lead to positive changes.

5. MIND AND SPEECH ARE TOOLS FOR CREATION:
Goddard highlights that we possess the tools of mind and speech, which are essential for creating our reality. Using these tools wisely can lead to the realization of our desires.

6. THE POWER OF REVISION:
The practice of revision involves reimagining and rewriting past experiences in a more idealistic way. This technique allows us to reshape our future by altering our past perceptions and reactions.

7. CHANGE INNER SPEECH AND CHANGE REALITY:
Our inner speech mirrors our mind, and our mind mirrors the creative power of God. Changing our inner speech and beliefs can lead to a transformation of our external reality.

8. LIVE IN THE MOMENT:
Goddard introduces the idea that time is not linear but rather curved. This means that our past, present, and future are interconnected. We have the power to change our past and present, thus shaping our future.

9. CONSCIOUSNESS LEADS TO AWAKENING:
Becoming conscious of our actions, thoughts, and inner conversations is the key to awakening. As we awaken, we see the world in a new light and understand our interconnectedness with others.

10. ENTER THE CIRCLE OF AWAKENED HUMANITY:
As we awaken, we enter a circle of awakened individuals who are in touch with their inner selves. This circle represents a higher level of awareness and understanding, leading to a more fulfilling life.

HOW TO USE YOUR IMAGINATION

By Neville Goddard | 1955

The following text is a transcription of a lecture.

The purpose of this record is to show you how to use your imagination to achieve your every desire. Most men are totally unaware of the creative power of a imagination and invariably bow before the dictates of "facts" and accepts life on the basis of the world without. But when you discover this creative power within yourself, you will boldly assert the supremacy of imagination and put all things in subjection to it. When a man speaks of God-in-man, he is totally unaware that this power called God-in-man is man's imagination. THIS is the creative power in man. There is nothing under heaven that is not plastic as potter's clay to the touch of the shaping spirit of imagination.

Once a man said to me, "You know, Neville, I love to listen to you talk about imagination, but as I do so, I invariably touch the chair with my fingers and push my feet into the rug just to keep my sense of the reality and the profundity of things. Well, undoubtedly he is still touching the chair with his fingers and pushing his feet into the rug.

Well, let me tell you of another one who didn't touch with her fingers and didn't push that foot of hers onto the board of the streetcar. It's the story of a young girl just turned seventeen. It was Christmas Eve, and she is sad of heart, for that year she had lost her father in an accident, and she is returning home to what seemed to be an empty house. She was untrained to do anything, so got herself a job as a waitress. This night it's quite late, Christmas Eve, it's raining, the car is full of laughing boys and girls home for their Christmas vacation, and she couldn't conceal the tears.

Luckily for her, as I said, it was raining, so she stuck her face into the heavens to mingle her tears with rain. And then holding the rail of the streetcar, this is what she did: she said, "This is not rain, why, this is spray from the ocean; and this is not the salt of tears that I taste, for this is the salt of the sea in the wind; and this is not San Diego, this is a ship, and I am coming into the Bay of Samoa." And there she felt the reality of all that she had imagined.

Then came the end of the journey and all are out.

Ten days later this girl received a letter from a firm in Chicago saying that her aunt, several years before when she sailed for Europe, deposited with them three thousand dollars with instructions that if she did not return to America, this money should be paid to her niece. They had just received information of the aunt's death and were now acting upon her instructions. One month later this girl sailed for Samoa. As she came into the bay it was late that night and there was salt of the sea in the wind. It wasn't raining, but there was spray in the air. And she actually felt what she'd felt one month before, only this time she had realized her objective.

Now, this whole record is technique. I want to show you today how to put your wonderful imagination right into the feeling of your wish fulfilled and let it remain there and fall asleep in that state. And I promise you, from my own experience, you will realize the state in which you sleep – if you could actually feel yourself right into the situation of your fulfilled desire and continue therein until you fall asleep.

As you feel yourself right into it, remain in it until you give it all the tones of reality, until you give it all the sensory vividness of reality. As you do it, in that state, quietly fall into sleep. And in a way you will never know – you could never consciously devise the means that would be employed – you will find yourself moving across a series of events leading you towards the objective realization of this state.

Now, here is a practical technique: The first thing you do, you must know exactly what you want in this world. When you know exactly what you want, make as life-like a representation as possible of what you would see, and what you would touch, and what you would do were you physically present and physically moving in such a state.

For example, suppose I wanted a home, but I had no money – but I still know what I want. I, without taking anything into consideration, I would make as life-like a representation of the home that I would like, with all the things in it that I would want. And then, this night, as I would go to bed, I would in a state, a drowsy, sleepy state, the state that borders upon sleep, I would imagine that I am actually in such a house, that were I to step off the bed, I would step upon the floor of that house, were I to leave this room, I would enter the room that is adjacent to my imagined room in that house. And while I am touching the furniture and feeling it to be solidly real, and while I am moving from one room to the other in my imaginary house, I would go to sound asleep in that state. And I know that in a way I could not consciously devise, I would realize my house. I have seen it work time and time again.

If I wanted promotion in my business I would ask myself, "What additional responsibilities would be mine were I to be given this great promotion? What would I do? What would I say? What would I see? How would I act? And then in my imagination I would begin to see and touch and do and act as I would outwardly see and touch and act were I in that position.

If I now desired the mate of my life, were I now in search of some wonderful girl or some wonderful man, what would I actually find myself doing that would imply that I have found my state? For instance, suppose now I was a lady, one thing I would definitely do, I would wear a wedding ring. I would take my imaginary hands and I would feel the ring that I would imagine to be there. And I would keep on feeling it and feeling it until it seemed to me to be solidly real. I would give it all the sensory vividness I am capable of giving anything. And while I am feeling my imaginary ring – which implies that I am married – I would sleep.

This story is told us in The Song of Songs, or A Song of Solomon:

It is said, "At night on my bed I sought him whom my soul loveth. I found him whom my soul loveth, and I would not let him go until I had brought him into my mother's house, right into the chamber of her that conceived me.

" If I would take that beautiful poem and put it into modern English, into practical language, it would be this: "While sitting in my chair I would feel myself right into the situation of my fulfilled desire, and having felt myself into that state I would not let it go. I would keep that mood alive, and in that mood I would sleep." That is taking it "right into my mother's chamber, into the chamber of her that conceived me."

You know, people are totally unaware of this fantastic power of the imagination, but when man begins to discover this power within him, he never plays the part that he formerly played. He doesn't turn back and become just a reflector of life; from here on in he is the affector of life. The secret of it is to center your imagination in the feeling of the wish fulfilled and remain therein. For in our capacity to live IN the feeling of the wish fulfilled lies our capacity to live the more abundant life. Most of us are afraid to imagine ourselves as important and noble individuals secure in our contribution to the world just because, at the very moment that we start our assumption, reason and our senses deny the truth of our assumption. We seem to be in the grip of an unconscious urge which makes us cling desperately to the world of familiar things and resist all that threatens to tear us away from our familiar and seemingly safe moorings.

Well, I appeal to you to try it. If you try it, you will discover this great wisdom of the ancients. For they told it to us in their own strange, wonderful, symbolical form.

But unfortunately you and I misinterpreted their stories and took it for history, when they intended it as instruction to simply achieve our every objective. You see, imagination puts us inwardly in touch with the world of states. These states are existent, they are present now, but they are mere possibilities while we think OF them. But they become overpoweringly real when we think FROM them and dwell IN them.

You know, there is a wide difference between thinking OF what you want in this world and thinking FROM what you want. Let me tell you when I first heard of this strange and wonderful power of the imagination. It was in 1933 in New York City. An old friend of mine taught it to me.

He turned to the fourteenth of John, and this is what he read: "In my father's house are many mansions. If it were not so, I would have told you. I go to prepare a place for you, and if I go and prepare a place for you, I will come again and receive you unto myself, that where I am there ye may be also." He explained to me that this central character of the Gospels was human imagination; that 'mansion' was not a place in some heavenly house, but simply my desire. If I would make a living representation of the state desired and then enter that state and abide in that state, I would realize it.

At the time I wanted to make a trip to the island of Barbados in the West Indies, but I had no money. He explained to me that if I would that night, as I slept in New York City, assume that I was sleeping in my earthly father's house in Barbados and go sound asleep in that state, that I would realize my trip. Well, I took him at his word and tried it. For one month, night after night as I fell asleep I assumed I was sleeping in my father's home in Barbados. At the end of my month an invitation from my family came inviting me to spend the winter in Barbados. I sailed for Barbados the early part of December of that year.

From then on I knew I had found this savior in myself. The old man told me that it would never fail. Even after it happened I could hardly believe that it would not have happened anyway. That's how strange this whole thing is. On reflection, it happens so naturally you begin to feel or to tell yourself, "Well, it would have happened anyway," and you quickly recover from this wonderful experience of yours.

It never failed me if I would give the mood, the imagined mood, sensory vividness. I could tell you unnumbered case histories to show you how it works, but in essence it is simple: You simply know what you want. When you know what you want, you are thinking of it. That is not enough. You must now begin to think FROM it. Well, how could I think from it? I am sitting here, and I desire to be elsewhere. How could I, while sitting here physically, put myself in imagination at a point in space removed from this room and make that real to me?

Quite easily. My imagination puts me in touch inwardly with that state. I imagine that I am actually where I desire to be. How can I tell that I am there? There is one way to prove that I am there, for what a man sees when he describes his world is, as he describes it, relative to himself. So what the world looks like depends entirely upon where I stand when I make my observation. So, if as I describe my world it is related to that point in space I imagine that I am occupying, then I must be there. I am not there physically, no, but I AM there in my imagination, and my imagination is my real self! And where I go in imagination and make it real, there I shall go in the flesh, also. When in that state I fall asleep, it is done. I have never seen it fail. So this is the simple technique upon how to use your imagination to realize your every objective.

Here is a very healthy and productive exercise for the imagination, something that you should do daily: Daily relive the day as you wish you had lived it, revising the scenes to make them conform to your ideals. For instance, suppose today's mail brought disappointing news. Revise the letter. Mentally rewrite it and make it conform to the news you wish you had received. Or, suppose you didn't get the letter you wish you had received. Write yourself the letter and imagine that you received such a letter.

Let me tell you a story that took place in New York not very long ago. In my audience sat this lady who had heard me, oh, numerous times, and I was telling the story of revision – that man, not knowing the power of imagination, he goes to sleep at the end of his day, tired and exhausted, accepting as final all the events of the day. And I was trying to show that man should, at that moment before he sleeps, he should rewrite the entire day and make it conform to the day he wished he had experienced.

Here is the way a lady wisely used this law of revision: It appears that two years ago she was ordered out of her daughter-in-law's home. For two years there was no correspondence. She had sent her grandson at least two dozen presents in that interval, but not one was ever acknowledged. Having heard the story of revision, this is what she did: As she retired at night, she mentally constructed two letters, one she imagined coming from her grandson, and the other from her daughter-in-law. In these letters they expressed deep affection for her and wondered why she had not called to see them.

This she did for seven consecutive nights, holding in her imaginary hand the letter she imagined she had received and reading these letters over and over until it aroused within her the satisfaction of having heard. Then she slept.

On the eighth day she received a letter from her daughter-in-law. On the inside there were two letters, one from her grandson and one from the daughter-in-law. They practically duplicated the imaginary letters that this grandmother had written to herself eight days before.

This art of revision can be used in any department of your life. Take the matter of health. Suppose you were ill. Bring before your mind's eye the image of a friend. Put upon that face an expression which implies that he or she sees in you that which you want the whole world to see. Just imagine he is saying to you that he has never seen you look better, and you reply, "I have never felt better."

Suppose your foot was injured. Then do this: Construct mentally a drama which implies that you are walking – that you are doing all the things that you would do if the foot was normal, and do it over and over and over until it takes on the tones of reality. Whenever you do in your imagination that which you would like to do in the outer world, that you WILL do in the outer world.

The one requisite is to arouse your attention in a way, and to such intensity, that you become wholly absorbed in the revised action. You will experience an expansion and refinement of the senses by this imaginative exercise and, eventually, achieve vision in the inner world.

The abundant life promised us is ours to enjoy now, but not until we have the sense of the creator as our imagination can we experience it.

Persistent imagination, centered in the feeling of the wish fulfilled, is the secret of all successful operations. This alone is the means of fulfilling the intention.

Every stage of man's progress is made by the conscious, voluntary exercise of the imagination. Then you will understand why all poets have stressed the importance of controlled, vivid imagination.

Listen to this one by the great William Blake:
In your own bosom you bear your heaven and earth,
And all you behold, though it appears without,
It is within, in your imagination,
Of which this world of mortality is but a shadow.

William Blake

Try it, and you too will prove that your Imagination is the Creator.

LESSONS FROM THE LECTURE

1. THE CREATIVE POWER OF IMAGINATION:
Neville Goddard underscores that many people underestimate the creative power of their imagination. Imagination is a potent tool for manifesting desires, and it can shape your reality.

2. BOLD ASSERTION OF IMAGINATION:
Once you realize the creative power within yourself, boldly assert the supremacy of imagination. Don't merely accept external circumstances; use your imagination to shape your world.

3. LIVE IN THE FEELING OF THE WISH FULFILLED:
To manifest your desires, immerse yourself in the feeling of your wish fulfilled. Fall asleep in that state, and you'll move towards the realization of your desires, often in ways you can't consciously anticipate.

4. CLEAR DEFINITION OF DESIRES:
Before applying imagination, have a precise understanding of what you want. Create a vivid mental representation of your desired state, making it as lifelike as possible.

5. THINKING FROM, NOT OF:
Shift from thinking "of" your desire to thinking "from" it. Imagine yourself already in the desired state and act, see, touch, and feel as if you are physically there. Your imagination is your real self.

6. REVISION OF PAST EVENTS:

Practice daily revision of past events. If something didn't go as desired, mentally rewrite it to align with your ideals. This helps reshape your perception and future experiences.

7. VISUALIZATION FOR HEALTH:

If you're facing health issues, use your imagination to visualize a healthy version of yourself. Mentally perform actions that imply good health, and eventually, your physical condition will align with your mental state.

8. EXPANSION OF SENSES:

Engage your imagination to refine and expand your senses. This imaginative exercise leads to an inner vision and enhances your perception of the world.

9. IMPORTANCE OF CONTROLLED IMAGINATION:

Controlled, vivid imagination is crucial for success. Poets like William Blake have emphasized this. When your imagination is under your control, you can shape your reality according to your desires.

10. PERSISTENT IMAGINATION: CONSISTENCY IS KEY.

Neville Goddard stresses the need for persistent imagination, focused on the feeling of the wish fulfilled. This is the secret to fulfilling your intentions and experiencing the abundant life.

BELIEVE IT IN

Neville 10-06-1969

The objective reality of this world is solely produced by the human imagination, in which all things exist. Tonight I hope to show you how to subjectively appropriate that which already exists in you, and turn it into an objective fact. Your life is nothing more than the out picturing of your imaginal activity, for your imagination fulfills itself in what your life becomes.

The last year that Robert Frost was with us, he was interviewed by Life Magazine and said: "Our founding fathers did not believe in the future, they believed it in." This is true. Having broken with England, our founding fathers could have established their own royalty here by making one of them the king, thereby perpetuating a royal family. They could have chosen a form of dictatorship, but they agreed to imagine a form of government that had not been tried since the days of the Greeks. Democracy is the most difficult form of government in the world, yet our founding fathers agreed to believe it in. They knew it would take place, because they knew the power of belief - the power I hope to show you that you are, tonight.

To say: "I am going to be rich," will not make it happen; you must believe riches in by claiming within yourself: "I am rich." You must believe in the present tense, because the active, creative power that you are, is God. He is your awareness, and God alone acts and is. His name forever and ever is "I am" therefore, he can't say: "I will be rich" or "I was rich" but "I am rich!"

Claim what you want to be aware of here and now, and - although your reasonable mind denies it and your senses deny it - if you will assume it, with feeling, your inward activity, established and perpetuated, will objectify itself in the outside world - which is nothing more than your imaginal activity, objectified. To attempt to change the circumstances of your life before you change its imaginal activity, is to labor in vain. This I know from experience. I had a friend who hated Roosevelt, yet wanted him to change. Every morning while shaving, my friend would tell Roosevelt off. He found great joy and satisfaction in this daily routine, yet could not understand why Roosevelt stayed the same. But I tell you, if you want someone to change, you must change your imaginal activity, for it is the one and only cause of your life. And you can believe anything in if you will not accept the facts your senses dictate; for nothing is impossible to imagine, and imagining - persisted in and believed - will create its own reality.

Now, all things exist in God, and he exists in you and you exist in him. Your eternal body is the human imagination, and that is God Himself. Your imagination is an actual body in which everything is contained. When you imagine, the thing itself comes out of that divine body, Jehovah. The story of Jesus is a wonderful mystery that cannot be solved until you discover, from experience, that he is your own wonderful human imagination.

We are told that God speaks to man in a dream and unveils himself in a vision. Now, vision is a waking dream like this room, while a dream occurs when you are not fully awake. A few years ago this vision was mine: I was taken in spirit into one of the early mansions on 5th Avenue in New York City at the turn of the century. As I entered, I saw that three generations were present and I heard the eldest man telling the others of their grandfather's secret. These are his words: "Grandfather used to say, while standing on an empty lot: `I remember when this was an empty lot.' Then he would paint a word picture of what he wanted to build there. He saw it vividly in his mind's eye as he spoke, and in time it was established. He went through life in that manner, objectively realizing what he had first subjectively claimed."

I tell you: everything in your outer world was first subjectively appropriated, I don't care what it is. Desire can be your empty lot where you may stand, remembering when that which you now have, was only a desire. If I now say: "I remember when I lectured at the Woman's Club in Los Angeles" I am implying I am no longer there, and am where I want to be. Remembering when you were poor, I have taken you out of poverty and placed you in comfort. I remember when you were sick, by taking you out of sickness and placing you in the state of health. I remember when you were unknown, implies you are now known. By changing my memory image of you, I can now remember when you, with all your fame and fortune, were unknown and broke. That was the secret of grandfather's success.

This is what I learned in vision. Do not put this thought aside because it came to me in vision. In the 12th chapter of the Book of Numbers it is said that God speaks to man through the medium of dreams and makes himself known through vision. If God makes himself known to you through vision, and speaks to you in dream, what is more important than to remember your dreams and visions? You can't compare the morning's paper or any book you may read, to your vision of the night, for that is an instruction from the depth of yourself.

God in you speaks to you in a dream, as he did to me when he took me on a trip in time to that beautifully staffed mansion at the turn of the century. As spirit, I was invisible to those present; but I heard more distinctly than they, and comprehended the words more graphically then they, because they had their millions; and who is going to tell one who already has millions how to get them. I entered their environment to hear their story, in order to share it with those who will hear and believe my words and then try it.

This doesn't mean that, just because you heard my vision you are going to enjoy wealth; you must apply what you heard, and remember when. If you would say: "I remember when I couldn't afford to spend $400 a month for rent," you are implying you can well afford it now. The words: "I remember when it was a struggle to live on my monthly income," implies you have transcended that limitation.

You can put yourself into any state by remembering when. You can remember when your friend expressed her desire to be married. By remembering when she was single, you are persuading yourself that your friend is no longer in that state, as you have moved her from one state into another.

When I say all things exist in the human imagination, I mean infinite states; for everything possible for you to experience now, exists in you as a state of which you are its operant power. Only you can make a state become alive. You must enter a state and animate it in order for it to outpicture itself in your world. You may then go back to sleep and think the objective fact is more real than its subjective state into which you have entered; but may I tell you: all states exist in the imagination. When a state is entered subjectively, it becomes objective in your vegetative world, where it will wax and wane and disappear; but its eternal form will remain forever and can be reanimated and brought back into being through the seed of contemplative thought. So I tell you: the most creative thing in you is to enter a state, and believe it into being.

Now, causation is the assemblage of mental states, which occurring creates that which the assemblage implies. Let us say that I have two friends who would empathize with me (not sympathize) if they heard my good news. I put them together and listen (all in my imagination) as they talk about me and what has happened in my life. Being true friends, I hear their words of joy and see their happiness reflected on their faces.

Then I allow myself to become visible to them and feel their handshake and embrace as I accept their congratulations as a fact. Now I have assembled a mental state, which occurring, created that which the assemblage implied; therefore I am its cause. As I walk, firmly believing in the reality of what I have done, and that imaginal act becomes a fact, I may question myself as it how it came about. Then, remembering my imaginal act I would say: "I did it." If I did it, then did not God do it? Yes, because God and I are one "I am".

Are you going to continue to believe there is another on the outside; or are you going to believe the great confession of faith, which I would urge you to accept? It's the great Sh'ma: "Hear O Israel, the Lord our God, the Lord is One." If the Lord is one he can't be two; therefore, if his name is I am and you say "1 am," you must be one with the Lord who brought the world into being.

Listen to these words: "By faith we understand that the world was created by the word of God, so that things that are seen were made out of things which do not appear." Here we see that the word of God is an imaginal activity, which -joined by faith - created the world. And faith is nothing more than the subjective appropriation of an objective hope. Now, when you discuss your desire with me, you cannot see my imaginal act relative to you. If you tell me you need a job and I accept that thought, when I think of you I remember your need.

But if I changed your words and heard you tell me you loved your job, I could remember when you needed one; for now my memory bank contains the fact that you have a job you like very much. And when we meet again you tell me that you have it, you are only bringing confirmation of my imaginal, creative act.

Now, if imagination works this way, and it proves itself in the testing time and time again, what does it matter what the world thinks? It costs you nothing to try it, and what a change in life it will produce for you. Try it, for you will prove it in performance.

This may be in conflict with what you believe God to be. Maybe you still want him to be someone on the outside, so that there are two of you and not one. That's all right if you do, but I tell you: God became you that there would not be you and God. He became you, that you may become God. If God became you, his name must be in you, and it is; for if I ask you anything, you must first be aware of the question before you can respond, and your awareness is God.

You may not be aware of who you are, where you are, or what you are; but you do know that you are. Aware of what your senses and reason dictate, you may believe that you are limited, unwanted, ignored, and mistreated; and your world confirms your belief in your imaginal activity.

And if you do not know that your awareness is causing this mistreatment, you will blame everyone but yourself; yet I tell you the only cause of the phenomena of life is an imaginal activity. There is no other cause.

If you believe in the horrors of the world as they are given to you in the paper and on television, your belief causes the horrors to continue. Believing the news of a shortage, you will buy what you do not need, blindly accepting the pressure to perpetuate an imaginal activity that keeps you frightened. All through scripture you are told to let not your heart be troubled, be not afraid, and fear not. If fear could be eliminated, there would be no need for psychologists or psychiatrists. It's a bunch of nonsense, anyway. Every day this branch of medicine changes their concepts and they are always in conflict as to what a man's attitude towards life is.

I say to everyone: the whole vast world is now in your human imagination, and you can bring any desire out of it by believing it into being.

First, you must know what you want, then create an image that fulfills it. Would your friends know and talk about it? Imagine they are with you now, discussing your fulfilled desire. You could be at a cocktail or dinner party that is being given in your honor. Or maybe it's a little get-together over tea.

Create a scene in your mind's eye and believe its reality in! That invisible state will produce the objective state you desire, for all objective reality is solely produced by imagination.

The clothes you are now wearing were first imagined. The chair in which you are seated, the room that surrounds you - there isn't a thing here that wasn't first imagined; so you can see that imagining creates reality. If you don't believe it, you are lost in a world of confusion.

There is no fiction. What is fiction today will be a fact tomorrow. A book written as a fictional story today comes out of the imagination of the one who wrote it, and will become a fact in the tomorrows. If you have a good memory or a good research system, you could find today's facts. Not every fact is recorded, because not every thought is written; yet every person imagines. A man, feeling wrongfully imprisoned and desiring to get even, will disturb the world, because all things by a law divine in one another's being, mingle. You can't stop the force that comes from one who is imagining, because behind the mask he wears, you and he are one. Start now to become aware of what you are thinking, for as you think, you imagine. Only then can you steer a true course to your definite end. If you lose sight of that end, however, you can and will be moved by seeming others. But if you keep your mind centered in the awareness of dwelling in your destination, you cannot fail.

The end of your journey is where your journey begins. When you tell me what you want, do not try to tell me the means necessary to get it, because neither you nor I know them. Just tell me what you want that I may hear you tell me that you have it. If you try to tell me how your desire is going to be fulfilled, I must first rub that thought out before I can replace it with what you want to be. Man insists on talking about his problems. He seems to enjoy recounting them and cannot believe that all he needs to do is state his desire clearly. If you believe that imagination creates reality, you will never allow yourself to dwell on your problems, for you will realize that as you do you perpetuate them all the more.

So I tell you: the greatest thing you can do is to believe a thing into existence, just as our founding fathers did. They had no current example of democracy. It existed in Greece centuries ago, but failed because the Greeks changed their imaginal activity. We could do that too. Don't think for one second we have to continue as a democracy. We could be under dictatorship within twenty-four hours, for everything is possible. If you like democracy, you must be constantly watchful to keep its concepts alive within you. It's the most difficult form of government. A man can voice an opinion and stage a protest here, but in other forms of government he cannot. If you want to enjoy the freedom of a democracy, you must keep it alive by being aware of it.

Now, if you keep this law, you don't have to broadcast what you want; you simply assume that you have it, for - although your reasonable mind and outer senses deny it - if you persist in your assumption your desire will become your reality. There is no limit to your power of belief, and all things are possible to him who believes. Just imagine what an enormous power that is. You don't have to be nice, good, or wise, for anything is possible to you when you believe that what you are imagining is true. That is the way to success.

I believe any man who has been successful in his life's venture has lived as though he were successful. Living in that state, he can name those who aided him in achieving his success; and he may deny that he was always aware of success, but his awareness compelled the aid he received.

To believe your desire into being is to exercise the wonderful creative power that you are. We are told in the very first Psalm: "Blessed is the man who delights in the law of the Lord. In all that he does, he prospers." This law, as explained in the Sermon on the Mount, is psychological. "You have heard it said of old, thou shalt not commit adultery, but I say unto you, anyone who lusts after a woman has already committed the act of adultery with her in his heart." Here we discover that it is not enough to restrain the impulse on the outside. Adultery is committed the moment the desire is thought!

Knowing what you want, gear yourself towards it, for the act was committed in the wanting. Faith must now be added, for without faith it is impossible to please God. Can you imagine a state and feel that your imaginal act is now a fact? It costs you nothing to imagine; in fact you are imagining every moment in time, but not consciously. But, may I tell you: if you use your creative power by imagining a desire is already fulfilled, when you get it, the circumstances will seem so natural that it will be easy to deny your imagination had anything to do with it, and you could easily believe that it would have happened anyway. But if you do, you will have returned to sleep once again.

First of all, most of us do not even realize our own harvest when it confronts us. And if we do remember that we once imagined it, reason will tell us it would have happened anyway. Reason will remind you that you met a man (seemingly by accident) at a cocktail party who was interested in making money. When he heard your idea, he sent you to see his friend, and look what happened - so really, it would have happened anyway. Then, of course, it is easy to ignore the law, but "Blessed is the man who delights in the law of the Lord. In all that he does he prospers."

Don't forget the law while you are living in the world of Caesar, and apply it wisely; but remember you are not justified by its use. Justification comes through faith. You must have faith in the incredible story that God promised to bring himself out of you, as you! This is God's promise to all, and all are asked to believe it. It is not what you are, but what you trust God to do, that saves you.

And to the degree that you trust God to save you, you will be saved. But he has given us a psychological law to cushion the inevitable blows of life. The law is simple: "As you sow, so shall you reap." It is the law of like begets like. As you imagine, so shall your life become. Knowing what you want, assume the feeling that would be yours if you had it. Persist in that feeling, and in a way you do not know and could not devise, your desire will become a fact. Grandfather made his fortune by standing on an empty lot and saying to himself: "I remember when this was an empty lot." Then he would paint a beautiful word picture of the structure he desired there. This is a wonderful technique. You can remember when you were unknown, penniless, and ill, or a failure. Remembering when you were, implies you are no longer that, and your power is in its implication.

Use the law and it will take you from success to success, as you conceive success to be. As far as I am concerned, success is to fulfill the promise, and you cannot do that through the law. The promise is fulfilled through faith. Are you holding true to the faith? Examine yourself to see if you are. I have told you an eternal story. Believe it, but do not change it. The story is this: God became you that you may become God. Use the law to cushion the blows while God keeps his promise; and then one day, when your journey is over, you will say: "Into thy hands I commit my spirit. Thou hast redeemed me, O Lord, faithful God." That's the cry on the cross. Commit your spirit to your imaginal act, relax and fall asleep knowing its redemption is assured. Then when you least expect it, God will prove to you that he has redeemed you by awakening in you, as you. Then you will be born, not of blood or of the will of the flesh, or of the will of man, but of God.

Now let us go into the silence.

LESSONS FROM THE LECTURE

1. IMAGINATION SHAPES REALITY:

Neville Goddard emphasizes that the objective reality we experience is a product of our imagination. Everything begins as a mental concept before manifesting in the physical world. Understanding the power of imagination is essential for creating the life you desire.

2. BELIEVE IN THE PRESENT TENSE:

Goddard highlights the importance of believing in the present tense. Your belief, or faith, is a creative force. You must declare your desires as if they are already true, using "I am" statements to harness the creative power within you.

3. CHANGE IMAGINAL ACTIVITY FIRST:

Before attempting to change external circumstances, it is crucial to change your internal imaginal activity. Your beliefs and thoughts are the primary drivers of your life experiences. Transform your inner world to see changes in your outer world.

4. DREAMS AND VISIONS ARE MESSAGES:

Goddard suggests that dreams and visions are means through which God communicates with individuals. Pay attention to your dreams and visions, as they may contain valuable insights and guidance for your life.

5. APPLYING THE LAW OF LIKE BEGETS LIKE:

The law of like begets like means that what you imagine and believe will become your reality. It emphasizes the importance of aligning your thoughts and beliefs with your desired outcomes.

6. REMEMBERING WHEN:

Goddard introduces the concept of "remembering when," where you reflect on a past state and imply that it has already changed. This technique can be used to shift from undesirable conditions to desired ones.

7. FAITH IS ESSENTIAL:

Faith is crucial in the process of manifesting your desires. It involves believing in the fulfillment of your desires even when external circumstances or evidence may suggest otherwise. Faith fuels the creative power within.

8. THE LAW OF GOD'S PROMISE:

Goddard suggests that God's promise to humanity is that individuals can become God by awakening to their divine nature. This awakening occurs through faith and aligning with the divine.

9. STAY ALIGNED WITH YOUR DESIRED STATE:

To manifest your desires, it's essential to stay aligned with your intended outcome and not focus on problems or obstacles. Maintain a clear mental image of your desired reality.

10. MIND YOUR THOUGHTS:

Be mindful of your thoughts and beliefs, as they have a direct impact on your reality. By controlling your thoughts and beliefs, you can shape your life in accordance with your desires.

AT YOUR COMMAND

Neville, 1939

Can man decree a thing and have it come to pass? Most decidedly he can! Man has always decreed that which has appeared in his world and is today decreeing that which is appearing in his world and shall continue to do so as long as man is conscious of being man. Not one thing has ever appeared in man's world but what man decreed that it should. This you may deny, but try as you will you cannot disprove it, for this decreeing is based upon a changeless principle. You do not command things to appear by your words or loud affirmations. Such vain repetition is more often than not confirmation of the opposite. Decreeing is ever done in consciousness. That is; every man is conscious of being that which he has decreed himself to be. The dumb man without using words is conscious of being dumb. Therefore he is decreeing himself to be dumb.

When the Bible is read in this light you will find it to be the greatest scientific book ever written. Instead of looking upon the Bible as the historical record of an ancient civilization or the biography of the unusual life of Jesus, see it as a great psychological drama taking place in the consciousness of man.

Claim it as your own and you will suddenly transform your world from the barren deserts of Egypt to the promised land of Canaan.

Every one will agree with the statement that all things were made by God, and without him there is nothing made that is made, but what man does not agree upon is the identity of God. All the churches and priesthoods of the world disagree as to the identity and true nature of God. The Bible proves beyond the shadow of a doubt that Moses and the prophets were in one hundred per cent accord as to the identity and nature of God. And Jesus' life and teachings are in agreement with the findings of the prophets of old. Moses discovered God to be man's awareness of being, when he declared these little understood words, "I AM hath sent me unto you." David sang in his psalms, "Be still and know that I AM God." Isaiah declared, "I AM the Lord and there is none else. There is no God beside me. I girded thee, though thou hast not known me. I form the light, and create darkness; I make peace, and create evil. I the Lord do all these things."

The awareness of being as God is stated hundreds of times in the New Testament. To name but a few: "I AM the shepherd, I AM the door; I AM the resurrection and the life; I AM the way; I AM the Alpha and Omega; I AM the beginning and the end"; and again, "Whom do you say that I AM?"

It is not stated, "I, Jesus, am the door. I, Jesus am the way," nor is it said, "Whom do you say that I, Jesus, am?" It is clearly stated, "I AM the way." The awareness of being is the door through which the manifestations of life pass into the world of form.

Consciousness is the resurrecting power – resurrecting that which man is conscious of being. Man is ever out-picturing that which he is conscious of being. This is the truth that makes man free, for man is always self-imprisoned or self-freed.

If you, the reader, will give up all of your former beliefs in a God apart from yourself, and claim God as your awareness of being – as Jesus and the prophets did – you will transform your world with the realization that, "I and my father are one." This statement, "I and my father are one, but my father is greater than I," seems very confusing – but if interpreted in the light of what we have just said concerning the identity of God, you will find it very revealing. Consciousness, being God, is as 'father.' The thing that you are conscious of being is the 'son' bearing witness of his 'father.' It is like the conceiver and its conceptions. The conceiver is ever greater than his conceptions yet ever remains one with his conception. For instance; before you are conscious of being man, you are first conscious of being. Then you become conscious of being man. Yet you remain as conceiver, greater than your conception – man.

Jesus discovered this glorious truth and declared himself to be one with God – not a God that man had fashioned. For he never recognized such a God. He said, "If any man should ever come, saying, 'Look here or look there,' believe them not, for the kingdom of God is within you."

Heaven is within you. Therefore, when it is recorded that "He went unto his father," it is telling you that he rose in consciousness to the point where he was just conscious of being, thus transcending the limitations of his present conception of himself, called 'Jesus.'

In the awareness of being all things are possible, he said, "You shall decree a thing and it shall come to pass." This is his decreeing – rising in consciousness to the naturalness of being the thing desired. As he expressed it, "And I, if I be lifted up, I shall draw all men unto me." If I be lifted up in consciousness to the naturalness of the thing desired I will draw the manifestation of that desire unto me. For he states, "No man comes unto me save the father within me draws him, and I and my father are one." Therefore, consciousness is the father that is drawing the manifestations of life unto you.

You are, at this very moment, drawing into your world that which you are now conscious of being. Now you can see what is meant by, "You must be born again." If you are dissatisfied with your present expression in life the only way to change it, is to take your attention away form that which seems so real to you and rise in consciousness to that which you desire to be. You cannot serve two masters, therefore to take your attention from one state of consciousness and place it upon another is to die to one and live to the other.

The question, "Whom do you say that I AM?" is not addressed to a man called 'Peter' by one called 'Jesus.' This is the eternal question addressed to one's self by one's true being. In other words, "Whom do you say that you are?" For your conviction of yourself – your opinion of yourself will determine your expression in life. He states, "You believe in God – believe also in me." In other words, it is the me within you that is this God.

Praying then, is seen to be recognizing yourself to be that which you now desire, rather than its accepting form of petitioning a God that does not exist for that which you now desire.

So can't you see why the millions of prayers are unanswered? Men pray to a God that does not exist. For instance: To be conscious of being poor and to pray to a God for riches is to be rewarded with that which you are conscious of being – which is poverty. Prayers to be successful must be claiming rather than begging – so if you would pray for riches turn from your picture of poverty by denying the very evidence of your senses and assume the nature of being wealthy.

We are told, "When you pray go within in secret and shut the door. And that which your father sees in secret, with that will he reward you openly." We have identified the 'father' to be the awareness of being. We have also identified the 'door' to be the awareness of being.

So 'shutting the door' is shutting out that which 'I' am now aware of being and claiming myself to be that which 'I' desire to be. The very moment my claim is established to the point of conviction, that moment I begin to draw unto myself the evidence of my claim.

Do not question the how of these things appearing, for no man knows that way. That is, no manifestation knows how the things desired will appear.

Consciousness is the way or door through which things appear. He said, "I AM the way" – not 'I,' John Smith, am the way, but "I AM," the awareness of being, is the way through which the thing shall come. The signs always follow. They never precede. Things have no reality other than in consciousness. Therefore, get the consciousness first and the thing is compelled to appear.

You are told, "Seek ye first the kingdom of Heaven and all things shall be added unto you." Get first the consciousness of the things that you are seeking and leave the things alone. This is what is meant by "Ye shall decree a thing and it shall come to pass."

Apply this principle and you will know what it is to 'prove me and see." The story of Mary is the story of every man. Mary was not a woman – giving birth in some miraculous way to one called 'Jesus.'

Mary is the awareness of being that ever remains virgin, no matter how many desires it gives birth to. Right now look upon yourself as this virgin Mary – being impregnated by yourself through the medium of desire – becoming one with your desire to the point of embodying or giving birth to your desire.

For instance: It is said of Mary (whom you now know to be yourself) that she know not a man. Yet she conceived. That is, you, John Smith, have no reason to believe that that which you now desire is possible, but having discovered your awareness of being to be God, you make this awareness your husband and conceive a man child (manifestation) of the Lord, "For thy maker is thine husband; the Lord of hosts is his name; the Lord God of the whole earth shall he be called." Your ideal or ambition is this conception – the first command to her, which is now to yourself, is "Go, tell no man." That is, do not discuss your ambitions or desires with another for the other will only echo your present fears. Secrecy is the first law to be observed in realizing your desire.

The second, as we are told in the story of Mary, is to "Magnify the Lord." We have identified the Lord as your awareness of being. Therefore, to 'magnify the Lord' is to revalue or expand one's present conception of one's self to the point where this revaluation becomes natural. When this naturalness is attained you give birth by becoming that which you are one with in consciousness.

The story of creation is given us in digest form in the first chapter of John.

"In the beginning was the word." Now, this very second, is the 'beginning' spoken of. It is the beginning of an urge – a desire. 'The word' is the desire swimming around in your consciousness – seeking embodiment. The urge of itself has no reality, For, "I AM" or the awareness of being is the only reality. Things live only as long as I AM aware of being them; so to realize one's desire, the second line of this first verse of John must be applied. That is, "And the word was with God." The word, or desire, must be fixed or united with consciousness to give it reality. The awareness becomes aware of being the thing desired, thereby nailing itself upon the form or conception – and giving life unto its conception – or resurrecting that which was heretofore a dead or unfulfilled desire. "Two shall agree as touching anything and it shall be established on earth."

This agreement is never made between two persons. It is between the awareness and the thing desired. You are now conscious of being, so you are actually saying to yourself, without using words, "I AM." Now, if it is a state of health that you are desirous of attaining, before you have any evidence of health in your world, you begin to FEEL yourself to be healthy. And the very second the feeling "I AM healthy" is attained the two have agreed. That is, I AM and health have agreed to be one and this agreement ever results in the birth of a child which is the thing agreed upon – in this case, health.

And because I made the agreement I express the thing agreed. So you can see why Moses stated, "I AM hath sent me." For what being, other than I AM could send you into expression? None – for "I AM the way – Beside me there is no other." If you take the wings of the morning and fly into the uttermost parts of the world or if you make your bed in Hell, you will still be aware of being. You are ever sent into expression by your awareness and your expression is ever that which you are aware of being.

Again, Moses stated, "I AM that I AM." Now here is something to always bear in mind. You cannot put new wine in old bottles or new patches upon old garments. That is; you cannot take with you into the new consciousness any part of the old man. All of your present beliefs, fears and limitations are weights that bind you to your present level of consciousness. If you would transcend this level you must leave behind all that is now your present self, or conception of yourself. To do this you take your attention away from all that is now your problem or limitation and dwell upon just being. That is; you say silently but feeling to yourself, "I AM. Do not condition this 'awareness' as yet. Just declare yourself to be, and continue to do so, until you are lost in the feeling of just being – faceless and formless. When this expansion of consciousness is attained, then, within this formless deep of yourself give form to the new conception by FEELING yourself to be THAT which you desire to be.

You will find within this deep of yourself all things to be divinely possible. Everything in the world which you can conceive of being, is to you, within this present formless awareness, a most natural attainment.

The invitation given us in the Scriptures is – "to be absent from the body and be present with the Lord." The 'body' being your former conception of yourself and 'the Lord' – your awareness of being. This is what is meant when Jesus said to Nicodemus, "Ye must be born again for except ye be born again ye cannot enter the kingdom of Heaven." That is; except you leave behind you your present conception of yourself and assume the nature of the new birth, you will continue to out-picture your present limitations.

The only way to change your expressions of life is to change your consciousness. For consciousness is the reality that eternally solidifies itself in the things round about you. Man's world in its every detail is his consciousness out-pictured. You can no more change your environment, or world, by destroying things than you can your reflection by destroying the mirror. Your environment, and all within it, reflects that which you are in consciousness. As long as you continue to be that in consciousness so long will you continue to out-picture it in your world.

Knowing this, begin to revalue yourself. Man has placed too little value upon himself. In the Book of Numbers you will read, "In that day there were giants in the land; and we were in our own sight as grasshoppers. And we were in their sight as grasshoppers." This does not mean a time in the dim past when man had the stature of giants. Today is the day, the eternal now when conditions round about you have attained the appearance of giants (such as unemployed, the armies of your enemy, your problems and all things that seem to threaten you) those are the giant that make you feel yourself to be a grasshopper. But, you are told, you were first, in your own sight a grasshopper and because of this you were to the giants – a grasshopper. In other words, you can only be to others what you are first to yourself. Therefore, to revalue yourself and begin to feel yourself to be the giant, a center of power, is to dwarf these former giants and make of them grasshoppers. "All the inhabitants of the earth are as nothing, and he doeth according to his will in the armies of Heaven and among all the inhabitants of the earth; and none can stay his hand, nor say unto him, "What doest thou'?" This being spoken of is not the orthodox God sitting in space but the one and only God – the everlasting father, your awareness of being. So awake to the power that you are, not as man, but as your true self, a faceless, formless awareness, and free yourself from your self imposed prison.

"I am the good shepherd and know my sheep and am known of mine. My sheep hear my voice and I know them and they will follow me." Awareness is the good shepherd. What I am aware of being, is the 'sheep' that follow me. So good a 'shepherd' is your awareness that it has never lost one of the 'sheep' that you are aware of being.

I am a voice calling in the wilderness of human confusion for such as I am aware of being, and never shall there come a time when that which I am convinced that I am shall fail to find me. "I AM" is an open door for all that I am to enter. Your awareness of being is lord and shepherd of your life. So, "The Lord is my shepherd; I shall not want" is seen in its true light now to be your consciousness. You could never be in want of proof or lack the evidence of that which you are aware of being.

This being true, why not become aware of being great; God-loving; wealthy; healthy; and all attributes that you admire?

It is just as easy to possess the consciousness of these qualities as it is to possess their opposites for you have not your present consciousness because of your world. On the contrary, your world is what it is because of your present consciousness. Simple, is it not? Too simple in fact for the wisdom of man that tries to complicate everything.

Paul said of this principle, "It is to the Greeks" (or wisdom of this world) "foolishness." "And to the Jews" (or those who look for signs) "a stumbling block"; with the result, that man continues to walk in darkness rather than awake to the being that he is. Man has so long worshipped the images of his own making that at first he finds this revelation blasphemous, since it spells death to all his previous beliefs in a God apart from himself. This revelation will bring the knowledge that "I and my father are one but my father is greater than I." You are one with your present conception of yourself. But you are greater than that which you are at present aware of being.

Before man can attempt to transform his world he must first lay the foundation – "I AM the Lord." That is, man's awareness, his consciousness of being is God. Until this is firmly established so that no suggestion or argument put forward by others can shake it, he will find himself returning to the slavery of his former beliefs. "If ye believe not that I AM he, ye shall die in your sins." That is, you shall continue to be confused and thwarted until you find the cause of your confusion. When you have lifted up the son of man then shall you know that I AM he, that is, that I, John Smith, do nothing of myself, but my father, or that state of consciousness which I am now one with does the works.

When this is realized every urge and desire that springs within you shall find expression in your world. "Behold I stand at the door and knock. If any man hear my voice and open the door I will come in to him and sup with him and he with me." The "I" knocking at the door is the urge.

The door is your consciousness. To open the door is to become one with that that which is knocking by FEELING oneself to be the thing desired. To feel one's desire as impossible is to shut the door or deny this urge expression. To rise in consciousness to the naturalness of the thing felt is to swing wide the door and invite this one into embodiment.

That is why it is constantly recorded that Jesus left the world of manifestation and ascended unto his father. Jesus, as you and I, found all things impossible to Jesus, as man. But having discovered his father to be the state of consciousness of the thing desired, he but left behind him the "Jesus consciousness" and rose in consciousness to that state desired and stood upon it until he became one with it. As he made himself one with that, he became that in expression.

This is Jesus simple message to man: Men are but garments that the impersonal being, I AM, the presence that men call God – dwells in. Each garment has certain limitations.

In order to transcend these limitations and give expression to that which, as man – John Smith – you find yourself incapable of doing, you take your attention away from your present limitations, or John Smith conception of yourself, and merge yourself in the feeling of being that which you desire. Just how this desire or newly attained consciousness will embody itself, no man knows. For I, or the newly attained consciousness, has ways that ye know not of; its ways are past finding out. Do not speculate as to the HOW of this consciousness embodying itself, for no man is wise enough to know the how. Speculation is proof that you have not attained to the naturalness of being the thing desired and so are filled with doubts.

You are told, "He who lacks wisdom let him ask of God, that gives to all liberally, and upbraideth not; and it shall be given unto him. But let him ask not doubting for he who doubts is as a wave of the sea that is tossed and battered by the winds. And let not such a one think that he shall receive anything from the Lord." You can see why this statement is made, for only upon the rock of faith can anything be established. If you have not the consciousness of the thing you have not the cause or foundation upon which thing is erected.

A proof of this established consciousness is given you in the words, "Thank you, father." When you come into the joy of thanksgiving so that you actually feel grateful for having received that which is not yet apparent to the senses, you have definitely become one in consciousness with the thing for which you gave thanks.

God (your awareness) is not mocked. You are ever receiving that which you are aware of being and no man gives thanks for something which he has not received. "Thank you father" is not, as it is used by many today a sort of magical formula. You need never utter aloud the words, "Thank you, father." In applying this principle as you rise in consciousness to the point where you are really grateful and happy for having received the thing desired, you automatically rejoice and give thanks inwardly. You have already accepted the gift which was but a desire before you rose in consciousness, and your faith is now the substance that shall clothe your desire.

This rising in consciousness is the spiritual marriage where two shall agree upon being one and their likeness or image is established on earth.

"For whatsoever ye ask in my name the same give I unto you." 'Whatsoever' is quite a large measure. It is the unconditional. It does not state if society deems it right or wrong that you should ask it, it rests with you. Do you really want it? Do you desire it? That is all that is necessary. Life will give it to you is you ask 'in his name.'

His name is not a name that you pronounce with the lips. You can ask forever in the name of God or Jehovah or Christ Jesus and you will ask in vain. 'Name' means nature; so, when you ask in the nature of a thing, results ever follow.

To ask in the name is to rise in consciousness and become one in nature with the thing desired, rise in consciousness to the nature of the thing, and you will become that thing in expression. Therefore, "what things soever ye desire, when ye pray, believe that ye receive them and ye shall receive them."

Praying, as we have shown you before, is recognition – the injunction to believe that ye receive is first person, present tense. This means that you must be in the nature of the things asked for before you can receive them.

To get into the nature easily, general amnesty is necessary. We are told, "Forgive if ye have aught against any, that your father also, which is in Heaven, may forgive you. But if ye forgive not, neither will your father forgive you." This may seem to be some personal God who is pleased or displeased with your actions but this is not the case.

Consciousness, being God, if you hold in consciousness anything against man, you are binding that condition in your world. But to release man from all condemnation is to free yourself so that you may rise to any level necessary; there is therefore, no condemnation to those in Christ Jesus.

Therefore, a very good practice before you enter into your meditation is first to free every man in the world from blame. For LAW is never violated and you can rest confidently in the knowledge that every man's conception of himself is going to be his reward. So you do not have to bother yourself about seeing whether or not man gets what you consider he should get. For life makes no mistakes and always gives man that which man first gives himself.

This brings us to that much abused statement of the Bible on tithing. Teachers of all kinds have enslaved man with this affair of tithing, for not themselves understanding the nature of tithing and being themselves fearful of lack, they have led their followers to believe that a tenth part of their income should be given to the Lord. Meaning, as they make very clear, that, when one gives a tenth part of his income to their particular organization he is giving his "tenth part" to the Lord – (or is tithing). But remember, "I AM" the Lord." Your awareness of being is the God that you give to and you ever give in this manner.

Therefore when you claim yourself to be anything, you have given that claim or quality to God. And your awareness of being, which is no respecter of persons, will return to you pressed down, shaken together, and running over with that quality or attribute which you claim for yourself.

Awareness of being is nothing that you could ever name. To claim God to be rich; to be great; to be love; to be all wise; is to define that which cannot be defined. For God is nothing that could ever be named.

Tithing is necessary and you do tithe with God. But from now on give to the only God and see to it that you give him the quality that you desire as man to express by claiming yourself to be the great, the wealthy, the loving, the all wise.

Do not speculate as to how you shall express these qualities or claims, for life has a way that you, as man, know not of. Its ways are past finding out. But, I assure you, the day you claim these qualities to the point of conviction, your claims will be honored. There is nothing covered that shall not be uncovered. That which is spoken in secret shall be proclaimed from the housetops. That is, your secret convictions of yourself – these secret claims that no man knows of, when really believed, will be shouted from the housetops in your world. For your convictions of yourself are the words of the God within you, which words are spirit and cannot return unto you void but must accomplish whereunto they are sent.

You are at this moment calling out of the infinite that which you are now conscious of being. And not one word or conviction will fail to find you.

"I AM" the vine and ye are the branches." Consciousness is the 'vine,' and those qualities which you are now conscious of being are as 'branches' that you feed and keep alive. Just as a branch has no life except it be rooted in the vine, so likewise things have no life except you be conscious of them. Just as a branch withers

and dies if the sap of the vine ceases to flow towards it, so do things in your world pass away if you take your attention from them, because your attention is as the sap of life that keeps alive and sustains the things of your world.

To dissolve a problem that now seems so real to you all that you do is remove your attention from it. In spite of its seeming reality, turn from it in consciousness. Become indifferent and begin to feel yourself to be that which would be the solution of the problem.

For instance; if you were imprisoned no man would have to tell you that you should desire freedom. Freedom, or rather the desire of freedom would be automatic. So why look behind the four walls of your prison bars? Take your attention from being imprisoned and begin to feel yourself to be free. FEEL it to the point where it is natural – the very second you do so, those prison bars will dissolve. Apply this same principle to any problem.

I have seen people who were in debt up to their ears apply this principle and in the twinkling of an eye debts that were mountainous were removed. I have seen those whom doctors had given up as incurable take their attention away from their problem of disease and begin to feel themselves to be well in spite of the evidence of their sense to the contrary. In no time at all this so called "incurable disease" vanished and left no scar.

Your answer to, "Whom do you say that I AM"? [sic] ever determines your expression. As long as you are conscious of being imprisoned or diseased, or poor, so long will you continue to out-picture or express these conditions.

When man realized that he is now that which he is seeking and begins to claim that he is, he will have the proof of his claim. This cue is given you in words, "Whom seek ye?" And they answered, "Jesus." And the voice said, "I am he." 'Jesus' here means salvation or savior. You are seeking to be salvaged from that which is not your problem.

"I am" is he that will save you. If you are hungry, your savior is food. If you are poor, your savior is riches. If you are imprisoned, your savior is freedom. If you are diseased, it will not be a man called Jesus who will save you, but health will become your savior. Therefore, claim "I am he," in other words, claim yourself to be the thing desired.

Claim it in consciousness – not in words – and consciousness will reward you with your claim. You are told, "You shall find me when you FEEL after me." Well, FEEL after that quality in consciousness until you FEEL yourself to be it. When you lose yourself in the feeling of being it, the quality will embody itself in your world.

You are healed from your problem when you touch the solution of it. "Who has touched me? For I perceive virtue is gone out of me." Yes, the day you touch this being within you – FEELING yourself to be cured or healed, virtues will come out of your very self and solidify themselves in your world as healings.

It is said, 'You believe in God. Believe also in me for I am he." Have the faith of God. "He made himself one with God and found it not robbery to do the works of God." Go you and do likewise. Yes, begin to believe your awareness, your consciousness of being to be God. Claim for yourself all the attributes that you have heretofore given an external God and you will begin to express these claims.

"For I am not a God afar off. I am nearer than your hands and feet – nearer than your very breathing." I am your awareness of being. I am that in which all that I shall ever be aware of being shall begin and end. "For before the world was I AM; and when the world shall cease to be, I AM; before Abraham was, I AM." This I AM is your awareness.

"Except the Lord build the house they labor in vain that build it." 'The Lord,' being your consciousness, except that which you seek is first established in your consciousness, you will labor in vain to find it. All things must begin and end in consciousness.

So, blessed indeed is the man that trusteth in himself – for man's faith in God will ever be measured by his confidence in himself. You believe in a God, believe also in ME.

Put not your trust in men for men but reflect the being that you are, and can only bring to you or do unto you that which you have first done unto yourself.

"No man taketh away my life, I lay it down myself." I have the power to lay it down and the power to take it up again.

No matter what happens to man in this world it is never an accident. It occurs under the guidance of an exact and changeless Law.

"No man" (manifestation) "comes unto me except the father within me draw him," and "I and my father are one." Believe this truth and you will be free. Man has always blamed others for that which he is and will continue to do so until he find himself as cause of all. "I AM" comes not to destroy but to fulfill. "I AM," the awareness within you, destroys nothing but ever fill full the molds or conception one has of one's self.

It is impossible for the poor man to find wealth in this world no matter how he is surrounded with it until he first claims himself to be wealthy. For signs follow, they do not precede. To constantly kick and complain against the limitations of poverty while remaining poor in consciousness is to play the fool's game. Changes cannot take place from that level of consciousness for life in constantly out-picturing all levels.

Follow the example of the prodigal son. Realize that you, yourself brought about this condition of waste and lack and make the decision within yourself to rise to a higher level where the fatted calf, the ring, and the robe await your claim.

There was no condemnation of the prodigal when he had the courage to claim this inheritance as his own. Others will condemn us only as long as we continue in that for which we condemn ourselves. So: "Happy is the man that condemneth himself not in that which he alloweth." For to life nothing is condemned. All is expressed.

Life does not care whether you call yourself rich or poor; strong or weak. It will eternally reward you with that which you claim as true of yourself.

The measurements of right and wrong belong to man alone. To life there is nothing right or wrong. As Paul stated in his letters to the Romans: "I know and am persuaded by the Lord Jesus that there is nothing unclean of itself, but to him that esteemeth anything to be unclean, to him it is unclean." Stop asking yourself whether you are worthy or unworthy to receive that which you desire. You, as man, did not create the desire. Your desires are ever fashioned within you because of what you now claim yourself to be.

When a man is hungry, (without thinking) he automatically desires food. When imprisoned, he automatically desires freedom and so forth. Your desires contain within themselves the plan of self-expression.

So leave all judgments out of the picture and rise in consciousness to the level of your desire and make yourself one with it by claiming it to be so now. For: "My grace is sufficient for thee. My strength is made perfect in weakness."

Have faith in this unseen claim until the conviction is born within you that it is so. Your confidence in this claim will pay great rewards. Just a little while and he, the thing desired, will come. But without faith it is impossible to realize anything. Through faith the worlds were framed because "faith is the substance of the thing hoped for – the evidence of the thing not yet seen."

Don't be anxious or concerned as to results. They will follow just as surely as day follows night.

Look upon your desires – all of them – as the spoken words of God, and every word or desire a promise. The reason most of us fail to realize our desires is because we are constantly conditioning them. Do not condition your desire. Just accept it as it comes to you. Give thanks for it to the point that you are grateful for having already received it – then go about your way in peace.

Such acceptance of your desire is like dropping seed – fertile seed – into prepared soil. For when you can drop the thing desired in consciousness, confident that it shall appear, you have done all that is expected to you. But, to be worried or concerned about the HOW of your desire maturing is to hold these fertile seeds in a mental grasp, and, therefore, never to have dropped them in the soil of confidence.

The reason men condition their desires is because they constantly judge after the appearance of being and see the things as real – forgetting that the only reality is the consciousness back of them.

To see things as real is to deny that all things are possible to God. The man who is imprisoned and sees his four walls as real is automatically denying the urge or promise of God within him of freedom.

A question often asked when this statement is made is; If one's desire is a gift of God how can you say that if one desires to kill a man that such a desire is good and therefore God sent? In answer to this let me say that no man desires to kill another. What he does desire is to be freed from such a one.

But because he does not believe that the desire to be free from such a one contains within itself the powers of freedom, he conditions that desire and sees the only way to express such freedom is to destroy the man – forgetting that the life wrapped within the desire has ways that he, as man, knows not of. Its ways are past finding out. Thus man distorts the gifts of God through his lack of faith.

Problems are the mountains spoken of that can be removed if one has but the faith of a grain of a mustard seed. Men approach their problem as did the old lady who, on attending service and hearing the priest say, "If you had but the faith of a grain of a mustard seed you would say unto yonder mountain 'be thou removed' and it shall be removed and nothing is impossible to you."

That night as she said her prayers, she quoted this part of the scriptures and retired to bed in what she thought was faith. On arising in the morning she rushed to the window and exclaimed: "I knew that old mountain would still be there."

For this is how man approaches his problem. He knows that they are still going to confront him. And because life is no respecter of persons and destroys nothing, it continues to keep alive that which he is conscious of being.

Things will disappear only as man changes in consciousness. Deny it if you will, it still remains a fact that consciousness is the only reality and things but mirror that which you are in consciousness.

So the heavenly state you are seeking will be found only in consciousness, for the kingdom of heaven is within you. As the will of heaven is ever done on earth you are today living in the heaven that you have established within you. For here on this very earth your heaven reveals itself. The kingdom of heaven really is at hand. NOW is the accepted time. So create a new heaven, enter into a new state of consciousness and a new earth will appear.

"The former things shall pass away. They shall not be remembered not come into mind any more. For behold, I," (your consciousness) "come quickly and my reward is with me."

I am nameless but will take upon myself every name (nature) that you call me. Remember it is you, yourself, that I speak of as 'me.' So every conception that you have of yourself – that is every deep conviction – you have of yourself is that which you shall appear as being – for I AM not fooled; God is not mocked.

Now let me instruct you in the art of fishing. It is recorded that the disciples fished all night and caught nothing. Then Jesus came upon the scene and told them to cast their nets in once more, into the same waters that only a moment before were barren – and this time their nets were bursting with the catch.

This story is taking place in the world today right within you, the reader. For you have within you all the elements necessary to go fishing. But until you find that Jesus Christ, (your awareness) is Lord, you will fish, as did these disciples, in the night of human darkness. That is, you will fish for THINGS thinking things to be real and will fish with the human bait – which is a struggle and an effort – trying to make contact with this one and that one: trying to coerce this being or the other being; and all such effort will be in vain. But when you discover your awareness of being to be Christ Jesus you will let him direct your fishing. And you will fish in consciousness for the things that you desire. For your desire – will be the fish that you will catch, because your consciousness is the only living reality you will fish in the deep waters of consciousness.

If you would catch that which is beyond your present capacity you must launch out into deeper waters, for, within your present consciousness such fish or desires cannot swim. To launch out into deeper waters, you leave behind you all that is now your present problem, or limitation, by taking your ATTENTION AWAY from it. Turn your back completely upon every problem and limitation that you now possess.

Dwell upon just being by saying, "I AM," "I AM," "I AM," to yourself. Continue to declare to yourself that you just are. Do not condition this declaration, just continue to FEEL yourself to be and without warning you will find yourself slipping the anchor that tied you to the shallow of your problems and moving out into the deep.

This is usually accompanied with the feeling of expansion. You will FEEL yourself expand as though you were actually growing. Don't be afraid, for courage is necessary. You are not going to die to anything by your former limitations, but they are going to die as you move away from them, for they live only in your consciousness. In this deep or expanded consciousness you will find yourself to be a power that you had never dreamt of before.

The things desired before you shoved off from the shores of limitation are the fish you are going to catch in this deep. Because you have lost all consciousness of your problems and barriers, it is now the easiest thing in the world to FEEL yourself to be one with the things desired.

Because I AM (your consciousness) is the resurrection and the life, you must attach this resurrecting power that you are to the thing desired if you would make it appear and live in your world. Now you begin to assume the nature of the thing desired by feeling, "I AM wealthy"; "I AM free"; "I AM strong." When these 'FEELS' are fixed within yourself, your formless being will take upon itself the forms of the things felt. You become 'crucified' upon the feelings of wealth, freedom, and strength. – Remain buried in the stillness of these convictions. Then, as a thief in the night and when you least expect it, theses qualities will be resurrected in your world as living realities.

The world shall touch you and see that you are flesh and blood for you shall begin to bear fruit of the nature of these qualities newly appropriated. This is the art of successful fishing for the manifestations of life.

Successful realization of the thing desired is also told us in the story of Daniel in the lion's den. Here, it is recorded that Daniel, while in the lion's den, turned his back upon the lions and looked towards the light coming from above; that the lions remained powerless and Daniel's faith in his God saved him.

This also is your story and you too must do as Daniel did. If you found yourself in a lion's den you would have no other concern but lions. You would not be thinking of one thing in the world but your problem – which problem would be lions.

Yet, you are told that Daniel turned his back upon them and looked towards the light that was his God. If we would follow the example of Daniel we would, while imprisoned within the den of poverty of sickness, take our attention away from our problems of debts or sickness and dwell upon the thing we seek.

If we do not look back in consciousness to our problems but continue in faith – believing ourselves to be that which we seek, we too will find our prison walls open and the thing sought – yes, "whatsoever things" – realized.

Another story is told us; of the widow and the three drops of oil. The prophet asked the widow, "What have ye in your house?" And she replied, "Three drops of oil." He then said to her, "Go borrow vessels. Close the door after ye have returned into your house and begin to pour." And she poured from three drops of oil into all the borrowed vessels, filling them to capacity with oil remaining.

You, the reader, are this widow. You have not a husband to impregnate you or make you fruitful, for a 'widow' is a barren state. Your awareness is now the Lord – or the prophet that has become your husband.

Follow the example of the widow, who instead of recognizing an emptiness or nothingness, recognized the something – three drops of oil.

Then the command to her, "Go within and close the door," that is, shut the door of the senses that tell you of the empty measures, the debts, the problems.

When you have taken your attention away completely by shutting out the evidence of the senses, begin to FEEL the joy, (symbolized by oil) – of having received the things desired. When the agreement is established within you so that all doubts and fears have passed away, then, you too will fill all the empty measures of your life and ill have an abundance running over.

Recognition is the power that conjures in the world. Every state that you have ever recognized, you have embodied. That which you are recognizing as true of yourself today is that which you are experiencing. So be as the widow and recognize joy, no matter how little the beginnings of recognition, and you will be generously rewarded – for the world is a magnified mirror, magnifying everything that you are conscious of being.

"I AM the Lord the God, which has brought thee out of the land of Egypt, out of the house of bondage; thou shalt have no other gods before me." What a glorious revelation, your awareness now revealed as the Lord thy God! Come, awake from your dream of being imprisoned. Realize that the earth is yours, "and the fullness thereof; the world, and all that dwells therein."

You have become so enmeshed in the belief that you are man that you have forgotten the glorious being that you are. Now with your memory restored DECREE the unseen to appear and it SHALL appear, for all things are compelled to respond to the Voice of God, Your awareness of being – the world is AT YOUR COMMAND!

LESSONS FROM THE LECTURE

1. AWARENESS OF BEING IS POWERFUL:
The central theme throughout the passages is the idea that one's awareness of being is a potent force. It is suggested that what you are conscious of being in your mind can be manifested in your life.

2. TITHING WITH GOD:
The concept of tithing is discussed as a way of giving to the Lord, but it is redefined to mean giving qualities or attributes to your own awareness of being. This emphasizes the idea that you can choose the qualities you want to express.

3. CLAIM YOUR DESIRES:
The passages emphasize the importance of claiming the qualities and attributes you desire for yourself. This involves believing in yourself and having faith in the power of your consciousness.

4. TURN AWAY FROM PROBLEMS:
When facing challenges or limitations, it is suggested that you should turn your attention away from them and focus on the desired outcomes. By doing so, you can dissolve problems and manifest solutions.

5. BELIEVE IN YOURSELF:
The passages stress the need to believe in yourself as a powerful being. Your faith in your own consciousness is essential for realizing your desires.

6. LET GO OF CONDITIONING:
Avoid conditioning your desires or placing limitations on them. Accept your desires as promises and give thanks for having already received them.

7. CHANGE IN CONSCIOUSNESS:
Changes in your life can only occur when there is a change in your consciousness. Shift your awareness to a higher level to manifest your desires.

8. LIVE IN THE END:
The idea of living in the end means feeling and embodying the qualities and conditions you desire as if you already have them. This helps bring them into your reality.

9. RECOGNIZE YOUR POWER:
Recognize the power of your own consciousness. You have the ability to create your reality and should not blame external factors for your circumstances.

10. THE WORLD MIRRORS YOUR CONSCIOUSNESS:
The world reflects what you are conscious of being. If you recognize joy and abundance within yourself, you will see these qualities mirrored in your external reality.

DISCLAIMER

Readers are advised not to perceive the information in this book as professional guidance. It serves as a reference and should be consulted after seeking advice from qualified professionals. The author is not liable for any charges, expenses, damages, or professional fees resulting from the application of the provided information.

While based on credible sources, the author cannot guarantee the accuracy and disclaims responsibility for omissions or inaccuracies. The primary purpose of the book is to educate and entertain.

Prior to adopting any tools or approaches suggested, readers are strongly encouraged to seek certified medical advice for healthcare procedures or treatments. This legal disclaimer applies whether the information is used directly or indirectly in cases of negligence, breach of contract, personal injuries, or other legal actions.

The text and images in this book are original and not copied from the source, representing an independent work.

COPYRIGHT

The publisher emphasizes that this book includes references to the original work for educational purposes. Both the editor and author fully acknowledge the original creator and their rights.

It is underscored that the reader's personal interpretation, as well as any misuse or unauthorized use of the material, is solely the reader's responsibility. While the book aims to provide accurate information, the editor does not commit to offering specialized services. It is strongly advised that readers consult an expert for assistance or guidance on the subject.

All rights are reserved for both the digital and printed versions. Reproduction of the content, whether in full or part, is strictly prohibited without the explicit consent of the author or publisher. Any form of reproduction, digital or analog, including photocopies, scans, electronic downloads, recordings, and translations, is forbidden for the entire book and its individual chapters.

Storing any part of this book in a retrieval system without explicit authorization is illegal, except for properly cited quotes in reviews or critical articles, where authorship must be verified. Reviews and critical articles must include citations detailing the source, book name, edition, author, publisher, and publication date, appropriately enclosed in quotation marks.

The Infinite Wealth Mindset - Unveiling The Spiritual And Mental Path To Infinite Wealth (Extended Edition)
By Neville Goddard

Author: Golden Oak Publishing and Neville Goddard
Contact: contact@goldenoakpublishing.com